Landscapes of
JERSEY

a countryside guide
Fifth edition

Geoff Daniel

D1342485

SUNFLOWER BOOKS

For Rik, with love

Fifth edition
Copyright © 2010
Sunflower Books™
PO Box 36160
London SW
www.sunfl

All rights re
No part of
may be rep
in a retrieva
transmitted
or by any m
electronic,
photocopy
or otherwis
prior writte
of the publ
Sunflower I
'Landscape
Registered Trademarks.

ISBN 978-1-85691-391-1

Rozel woods (Walk 9 and Picnic 9)

Important note to the reader

I have tried to ensure that the descriptions and maps in this book are error-free at press date. The book is updated, where necessary, whenever future printings are undertaken. It will be very helpful for me to receive your comments (sent in care of the publishers, please) for the updating of future editions. I also rely on those who use this book — especially walkers — to use their common sense as well. Natural hazards are few in Jersey, but use good judgement when walking on cliff-tops in windy conditions, and allow plenty of time when exploring sea caves or beaches at low tide. The rising tide flows very quickly and can trap the unwary. Jersey does *not* have an extensive public footpath network: some tracks may look public, but are in fact on private land. I believe that all the walks in this book are on public roads, tracks and paths, but if you discover otherwise, please respect the wishes of the landowner. Abiding by the country code (page 23) is wise in any event.

Cover photograph: sculpture near the Corbière lighthouse commemorating the rescue of passengers from the ferry St Malo in 1995 (Walk 4 and Picnic 4)

Photographs by the author, with the exception of pages 2, 10, 11, 14, 16, 18, 20, 33, 36 (bottom), 39, 40, 44, 49, 50, 51, 55, 59 and cover (John Seccombe), 17 (Jersey Goldsmiths), 36 (top) (Pallot Heritage Steam Museum) and 57 (Jersey War Tunnels).
Maps based upon the 1:25,000 map prepared by the Ordnance Survey for the Island Development Committee (1981), reproduced with the permission of the IDC. Crown/IDC copyright reserved. The maps have been updated to reflect important changes.
A catalogue record for this book is available from the British Library.
Printed and bound in Great Britain by Brightsea Press, Exeter

● Contents

Preface   4

Getting about   7

Picnicking   9

Touring   12

    THE WAY WEST   14
      St Helier • St Aubin • Noirmont • La Corbière • L'Etacq
      • Grosnez • La Grève de Lecq • Devil's Hole • Lion Park
      • Jersey War Tunnels (German Underground Military
      Hospital) • St Lawrence • Millbrook • St Helier

    THE EAST END   18
      St Helier • Sion • Pallot Steam Museum • (Bouley Bay) •
      Jersey's zoo • Rozel • St Catherine's Bay • Mont Orgueil
      • La Hougue Bie • La Rocque • Green Island • St Helier

Walking   22
  Where to stay   22
  Weather   22
  What to take   23
  A country code for walkers and motorists   23
  Waymarking and maps   24

    THE WALKS
    The walks (all circular except 7 and 11) are arranged starting with
    coastal walks running clockwise round the island from St Helier,
    followed by four inland walks. The symbol ➡ indicates short circular
    walks which are especially suitable for motorists.

    1 St Helier heritage ➡   25
    2 St Brelade • Beau Port • La Lande du L'Ouest •
       Corbière • ➡   29
    3 Noirmont and Portelet Bay ➡   32
    4 The Corbière walk   35
    5 Le Val de la Mare (Short walk ➡)   37
    6 The Pinnacle ➡   40
    7 The north coast   42
    8 Sorel and La Vallée des Mouriers ➡   45
    9 Round St Martin's and Rozel   46
    10 A short stroll around Flicquet ➡   50
    11 St Catherine's to Gorey   52
    12 St Lawrence: the heart of Jersey   53
    13 Jersey War Tunnels (German Underground Hospital)   56
    14 Gorey village and Queen's Valley (Short walk) ➡   58
    15 La Hougue Bie (Short walk ➡)   60

Buses and inter-island transport   62
St Helier town plan   25
Index   64
Island touring map   *inside back cover*

3

Preface

When you invest a little of your time and curiosity in Jersey, it feels much larger than only 45 square miles.

For the walker, Jersey expands with every step, for there is so much visual enjoyment and so much history to stir the imagination. Each bay, each stretch of cliff-top has a story to tell ... and each mile of country lane whispers secrets of its own.

To the motorist, a distance on paper means very little when translated to miles or kilometres per hour on this island, for whichever route is planned, there will be many a reason to stop and enjoy scenery, watering hole, or man-made attraction.

The picnicker is spoiled for choice of sites, whether opting for an official site with barbecue facilities or simply settling for a quiet spot along a walk route.

Landscapes of Jersey has been written for countryside enthusiasts. You will not find details of restaurants, hotels, shop opening hours, or other conventional guide book information here: these subjects are amply covered in a free guide given to all visitors when they arrive at the port or airport (or you can log on to the official website: www.jersey.com, in advance). Instead, I've concentrated on giving clear instructions for the car tours and walks, with some of my personal observations that may add interest to your exploration.

Whether you are a walker, a motorist, or simply taking a family holiday, you are assured of a warm Jersey welcome and if not a guarantee, then at least a fair chance of good weather. The Gulf Stream washes all the Channel Islands, and Jersey in particular has an excellent sunshine record, well above the UK average. Jersey's climate has been compared with that of southern Cornwall but drier and warmer. Even in winter, frosts are rare and snow even rarer. No matter what season it is, photographers will appreciate the quality of light in Jersey on any clear day.

Jersey's past
Invasion in one form or another has been a key factor in Jersey's history for a thousand years.

In the 9th century Viking raiders plundered all the Channel Islands, regarding them as a bonus on pillaging

Chusan palm (Trachycarpus fortunei) *seen during Walk 4 to Corbière. Palm trees come as no surprise: Jersey's climate has been compared with that of southern Cornwall, but even warmer.*

voyages to Britain and France.

Between the 13th and 15th centuries, France repeatedly tried to regain control of what was once theirs, for the islands were (and still are) part of the Duchy of Normandy. The then Duke of Normandy, King John, relinquished the mainland duchy to France in 1204, so the Channel Islands are, in fact, all that remain of the Duchy of Normandy; the Queen is the Duke of Normandy (one of her oldest titles).

In the Napoleonic era, France sided with the American colonists in their fight for independence and thus declared war on Britain. This resulted in defensive towers going up around Jersey (some are Martello towers, others are more accurately described as 'Jersey round towers', but they are similar in appearance).

Most recently, Jersey was occupied for five years during World War II by Nazi forces (see the Noirmont walk on page 32 and Jersey War Tunnels on page 56). But oddly, though concrete bunkers and towers proliferate, they seem to add a dimension to the landscape, rather than ruin it.

Jersey's present

The island's independent government of elected representatives is known as *Les Etats* — the States of Jersey. This refers to the three estates — the Court, the Church and the People. The President and Speaker is the Bailiff, appointed by the Crown. The *Vicomte* (sheriff) carries the Royal Mace (the gift of King Charles II), the symbol of the Bailiff's authority. The Bailiff is also the President and Chief Judge of the Royal Court, where he is assisted by *Jurats* (honorary magistrates). Law officers are appointed by the Crown; they may speak but not vote. The

Lieutenant Governor represents the Queen; he may attend, but takes no part in debates.

Much of what you see will be familiar to British visitors. Indeed, many Britons have settled in Jersey (not easy now, because of strict residential qualifications). However, scores of roads and streets have French names, while the Jersey accent derives from a time when the Jersey-Norman patois was more widely used than it is now. It is plain fact that for all Jersey's historical antipathy to France, the French mainland is easily visible on most days ... a mere 17 miles away.

Jersey's reputation as a financial centre is well known: some 50 major banks and finance houses are based on the island. Income tax is low (20%), and while UK VAT does not apply, a local general sales tax (GST; currently 3%) is added to the price of goods. Some shopkeepers absorb or waive the GST, particularly when charging the full UK price (including VAT), citing transport costs to make up the difference. But other shopkeepers deduct VAT, so look for competitive pricing. You can use UK currency on the island, but you'll often receive change in Jersey notes (£1, £5 or £10) or coins. Jersey notes can be exchanged free of commission at any UK bank.

Acknowledgements

I am indebted to the following for help in researching and preparing this book:

The States of Jersey Island Development Committee;

Howard B Baker of St Helier, whose intimate knowledge of Jersey, warmly shared, was of immense value, and whose own reference map 'The German Occupation of Jersey 1940/45' was a thorough and revealing document on the island's wartime experience;

Jersey Tourism, for information, hospitality and mobility;

Mike Freeman, States of Jersey Conservation Department, for information on Jersey's natural history;

The Jersey Society (La Société Jersiaise) for use of its library;

Channel Islands Occupation Society;

Sue Hardy, who has checked recent editions of the book, and who devised Walk 12 featuring the Millennium Path in St Lawrence which was created in the year 2000.

Books

Landscapes of Jersey is primarily a guide to countryside exploration and is intended to be used in tandem with a standard guide. Many more locally-published books on specific subjects such as bird watching or the Occupation years (or indeed, other walking guides) may be found in St Helier bookshops and many island newsagents and gift shops.

Also of interest

Landscapes of Guernsey (with Alderney, Sark and Herm) a companion book to this one, also published by Sunflower Books.

Getting about

A **hired car** is the most practical way of exploring Jersey, though by no means the only way. There is a wide choice of makes and models, and most vehicles are brand new. Hire vehicles are distinguished on the island by the prefix letter 'H' on the car's number plate. You can also take your own car, but a caravan or camper van may only be driven from ferry to camp site at a prebooked time and there are size restrictions.

To be able to hire a car, visitors must provide a valid driving licence with no endorsements for dangerous driving or drink/driving within the past five years. (Holders of photocard licences must also have the paper form D470 with them.) Drivers must be over 20 years of age, but there is no upper age limit (subject to any hire car insurance company proviso). Collision damage waiver is not compulsory but, if you do not take this option, you may be asked for a hefty deposit to cover part of the insurance excess (sometimes £500 or more), and this amount would become your responsibility in the event of damage to the car. It's up to you whether you pay the extra for CDW and peace of mind. Do shop around for car hire: some firms allow a useful discount provided you book with them direct rather than through an agent or a hotel.

Motor cycles, **mopeds** and **scooters** can also be hired; the wearing of crash helmets by rider and pillion passenger is compulsory.

Petrol carries slightly less duty than in the UK and is therefore marginally cheaper. On the fold-out touring map and in the touring notes, I have not attempted to list the location of every filling station, because there are so many; it would be difficult to drive five miles without seeing one! (Likewise, although the touring map indicates the locations of some cafés, restaurants and attractions, it is by no means comprehensive in this respect, and you will come across many more.)

Parking places and official car parks are plentiful; many are free of charge (most parking is free of charge between 5pm and 8am). At paying parks, you cannot pay cash but must display scratch paycards, on which you indicate date and time of arrival. These are sold by garages and many shops. Even at the height of the season, it's not difficult to find parking space, except perhaps in the main car parks in St Helier (or areas set aside for residents' parking). However, it is usually easy to find a space in the huge Pier Road multi-storey park, only five or six minutes' walk from St Helier centre. There are a few limited-waiting parking places in St Helier, some needing a paycard, others permitting free parking with a parking disc. The latter is sometimes provided with a hire car. If not, you can purchase one at the Town Hall, Motor Traffic Office, or at post offices. (If you do not have a parking disc, it is permissible to use a paycard instead in any parking disc area.) But you'll find free parks all over the island where you'll need neither disc nor paycard.

There is an all-island **maximum speed restriction** of 40mph/64kph, but in many places the limit is less than this, sometimes as low as 15mph/24kph. Places and junctions where you must halt are indicated by a yellow line across the road. A single yellow line parallel with the kerb or pavement means no waiting at all (the equivalent of a double yellow line in the UK). There are many roundabouts with a 'filter in turn' system — watch out for the signs. At these, one vehicle at a time enters the roundabout from each road joining it, everyone taking their 'turn'. It can be a bit confusing when you are not used to it, but it works!

Some country roads are designated '**green lanes**' with a 15mph speed limit for safer walking and cycling. Special road signs alert motorists using these routes.

Buses operate throughout the island from a central bus and coach station at Liberation Square, St Helier. There's a very frequent service to popular centres such as St Aubin and Gorey, but the service to more distant points is also good, and especially useful for walkers doing sections of the north coast path. See pages 62-63.

Cyclists are catered for by several cycle hire depots, and bicycles can be hired for a day or by the week.

Taxi ranks can be found at the airport and in St Helier, and there are numerous private hire companies operating. There are set tariffs, with fares clearly shown on a meter, and with different tariffs applying to day and night hire, and on public holidays.

Coaches offering day and half-day excursions are run by Tantivy Blue Coaches and Waverley Coaches.

Excursions to the other Channel Islands or day trips to France can be made by sea or air; see page 63.

☀ Picnicking

Picnicking is a particular pleasure in Jersey, where there are so many suitable settings. I have chosen some of my favourites; many are accessible by bus, as well as by car or bicycle. Jersey can be breezy — check the wind direction before choosing your picnic place!

All the information you need to get to these picnic spots is given below, where *picnic numbers correspond to walk numbers*. Beside the picnic title you'll find a map reference: the exact location of the picnic spot is shown on this *walking map* with the symbol **P**. I also include transport details (🚐 = how to get there by bus; 🚗 = where to park), how long a walk you will have, and any other information you might find useful. Some picnic sites have tables (and sometimes griddles); these are indicated by a ⊟ in the list below and on the touring map.

Ready-prepared picnic fare can be obtained at Marks & Spencers in St Helier or at St Brelade (Red Houses), but patronise the local shops as well: try the take-aways at one of the numerous outlets in St Helier — around the market and along The Esplanade near the bus station.

Please remember that if more than a few minutes' walking is required, you will need to wear **sensible shoes** and to take a **sunhat** (○ indicates a picnic in full sun). A plastic groundsheet also comes in handy, in case the ground is damp or prickly.

1 ELIZABETH CASTLE (touring map and St Helier plan page 25; photograph page 28) ○

🚐 by bus: 30min on foot. Bus to St Helier.
🚗 by car: up to 30min on foot. Park in St Helier (paycard required).
Reached on foot by causeway at low tide from opposite the Grand Hotel (or you can ride across in one of the amphibious vehicles). *Picnic in the castle grounds (where there are plenty of benches). Allow 2 hours if you decide to visit the museums (admission charge).*

2 BEAU PORT (map pages 30-31; photograph page 11) ○

🚐 by bus: 20-30min on foot. Bus 12 to St Brelade's Bay. From St Brelade's Church (see map) take the signposted footpath to the bay.
🚗 by car: Park at the free car park above Beau Port Bay, reached on narrow roads signposted from St Brelade's Church or by the first left turn just after turning onto the B83 road to Corbière. (Picnic spots near the car park; or allow 10-20min to get down to the beach.)
A beautiful, unspoiled little bay, really gorgeous on a warm, clear evening. Sit on grassy banks or sand.

The extensive dunes of Les Mielles: a maze of paths with many picnic places, both official and impromptu (Picnic 5a; near Walk 5)

3 NOIRMONT (map pages 30-31; photographs pages 15 and 34) ○

🚌 by bus: 10min on foot. Bus 12a to Portelet. From the terminus take the cliff-top path in the corner of the car park overlooking the bay. This will lead you through gorse and heather to Noirmont Point.
🚗 by car: under 5min on foot. Park at Noirmont (ample free parking).
Dazzling views of the coastline and St Helier from this striking headland.
�架 *nearby.*

4 LA CORBIERE (map pages 30-31; photograph page 17) ○

🚌 by bus: up to 15min on foot. Bus 12 to La Corbière.
🚗 by car: up to 15min on foot. Park at La Corbière (free).
Stunning views from this exposed southwest corner; enjoy a stroll to the lighthouse. Some benches at viewpoints, nice grassy spots.

5a LA MIELLE DE MORVILLE (touring map; photograph above) ⊼

🚌 by bus: up to 5min on foot. Bus 12a to La Mielle de Morville.
🚗 by car: up to 5min on foot. Park at La Mielle de Morville, just off the road behind St Ouen's Bay (free).
Three organised picnic sites with barbecues, or scores of places in the dunes. There are information boards about nature trails and bird hides overlooking the pools of water.

5b LE VAL DE LA MARE (map page 37; photograph page 38)

🚌 by bus: 30min on foot. Bus 9 to Val de la Mare car park.
🚗 by car: 30min on foot. Free parking at Val de la Mare on the A12.
Follow Walk 5 (page 37) for 15min, but turn *right*, to skirt the western arm of the reservoir for a further 15min.
Grassy slopes and convenient benches; splendid views over St Ouen's Bay. Shade from trees nearby.

6 THE PINNACLE (map on reverse of touring map; photographs page 41 and cover) ○

🚌 by bus: up to 20min on foot. Bus 12a to L'Etacq (terminus).
🚗 by car: up to 20min on foot. Park at Le Grand Etacquerel (free).
Follow Walk 6 (pages 40-41) from Le Grand Etacquerel (the L'Etacq bus terminus); note that there are some steep gradients.
Magnificent (but isolated) cliff-top setting. Do not climb down the slopes, as cliff erosion has made this hazardous. Stout shoes essential.

7a RONEZ (map on reverse of touring map) ⊼ ○

🚗 by car: up to 5min on foot. Park free at the site, on the north coast east of Ronez Quarry (well signposted opposite La Fontaine Tavern).
Three grills in two areas, one in a loop of the road (useful for parking), the other two below the road (better coastal views).

7b BOULEY BAY (map on reverse of touring map) ○

🚌 by bus: up to 30min on foot. Bus 4 to Trinity Church, then take the (signposted) road to Bouley Bay.

🚗 by car: up to 20min on foot. Park (free) on the jetty just to the west of the bay (access is via the narrow C96, north of Trinity Church).

Picnic at Le Parcq de la Petite Falaise (a little country park) for superb views, or on the beach. Otherwise walk up the fairly steep track to Le Jardin d'Olivet, the scene of a battle in 1549.

9 ROZEL WOODS (map page 47; photographs pages 2 and 20)

🚗 by car: 10min on foot. See page 46 for free parking details.

Follow Walk 9 (page 46) into the woods, past the small pond. *Benches available; good shade.*

11a ARCHIRONDEL (map page 47) 🎑

🚗 by car: up to 10min on foot. Park at Archirondel Tower (free).

Two barbecue areas lie off the B29 north of the tower. Shade nearby.

11b ANNE PORT (map page 47) 🎑 ○

🚗 by car: no walking. Park at the site (B29, north of Mont Orgueil).

Fine views from this headland at the north end of the little bay. Tables, but no barbecues.

12 WATERWORKS VALLEY (map page 54) 🎑

🚗 by car: no walking. Two picnic spots (free parking) on the C119.

Tree-lined countryside near the reservoirs. Benches, but no tables.

14 QUEEN'S VALLEY RESERVOIR (map page 47; photograph page 59)

🚌 by bus: 15min on foot. Bus 3a to St Saviour's Hospital.

🚗 by car: 15min on foot. Park at the St Saviour's Hospital end of the Queen's Valley Reservoir (free).

Follow the path along the eastern bank of the lake, until you reach the causeway. Pass it and, under 5min later, climb a couple of steps to a grassy bank with pleasant views over the lake. Shade nearby.

15 LA HOUGUE BIE (map page 60) 🎑

🚌 by bus: no walking. Bus 3a to La Hougue Bie.

🚗 by car: no walking. Park at La Hougue Bie (free).

No barbecues, but much to see: large underground neolithic/megalithic chamber, medieval chapels, geological and archaeological exhibits, wartime memorial in underground bunker. Drinks available; ample shade.

The delightful little bay of Beau Port (Car tour 2, Walk 2 and Picnic 2)

❀ Touring

Jersey is an island roughly nine miles by five (15km by 8km), with about 450 miles of good, if sometimes narrow roads. Exploring this road network will take more time than you might imagine: not only is there is much to see and do en route, but there is an **island-wide speed limit of 40mph/64kmph** (even less in some places). And rightly so. This is not an island to be taken in a hurry. However you put together your day, it would be difficult not to enjoy it in Jersey.

Most visitors like to hire a car for their stay on the island. You can take your own car if you wish, by conventional car ferry from Portsmouth or by high speed 'Wavepiercer' catamaran from either Weymouth or Poole in Dorset. Drink-driving and seat-belt laws are similar to those in the rest of Britain and are keenly enforced, especially drink-driving laws. Visiting drivers **must** carry their licence (if you have a photocard licence you must have the paper form D470 as well). For further information on car hire and driving on the island, see page 7.

The touring notes are brief: they include little information readily available in standard guides. Instead, I concentrate on taking you to my favourite natural and man-made attractions, and I emphasise possibilities for **picnicking** and **walking**, with a good selection of circular walks for motorists (see Contents, page 3).

The pull-out touring map is designed to be held out opposite the touring notes. This map deliberately omits many of the lesser roads, but all the roads I would recommend for car touring are included, and you may find it easier to use while motoring than some of the free give-away maps that are available at the port or airport. When motoring near a walk (indicated by large green numbers), you may wish to use the touring map in tandem with the 1:25,000 Ordnance Survey map extracts printed in the book.

With almost 450 miles of road to explore, a few suggestions may be useful. You can do a circuit quite easily and take your choice of north-south routes along several picturesque valleys. Moreover, by creating a circuit using coast road and central valley, you will see the best of Jersey. But beware: east-west tours across the middle of the island are a different matter, and it is very easy to lose your sense of direction and find yourself driving round in circles! Unless you know the lanes intimately, you are almost certain to get lost.

I offer two main route suggestions with optional side-tracks to take in some of the more popular attractions. I need hardly say that while references to things to see and

do are correct at the time of writing, changes can take place at very short notice — businesses change hands; authorities may change opening hours or restrict access. So, if there's something I have highlighted that you would particularly like to see, do check with the Jersey Tourism office, or telephone the attraction you plan to visit, before making a special journey.

Cumulative distances are given from St Helier (see town plan, page 25). A **key to the symbols** in the notes is on the touring map.

The gorgeous sweep of Gorey Harbour, seen from the castle at the top of Mont Orgueil (Car tour 2, Walk 11)

Car tour 1: THE WAY WEST

St Helier • St Aubin • Noirmont • La Corbière • L'Etacq • Grosnez • La Grève de Lecq • Devil's Hole • Jersey War Tunnels (German Underground Military Hospital) • St Lawrence • Millbrook • St Helier

36mi/58km; about 2-3 hours' driving plus time for visits en route

On route: ⩎ at Noirmont, La Mielle de Morville, L'Etacq; Picnics (see pages 9-11): (2), 3, 4, 5a, (5b), 6, (7), 12; Walks (2), 3, 4, (5) 6, 7, (8), 12, 13

All roads on this route are in excellent condition, but be prepared for a few hairpin bends and some very narrow lanes. Watch your speed!

From St Helier, head out on the Esplanade following the signs to **St Aubin★** (3mi ✝⛰⌂✕🍴☕WC), a quieter resort area than St Helier, with a delightful harbour. Keep to the narrow harbour road out of St Aubin, then turn sharp right at The Old Court House Hotel. It's a very narrow road here, through a series of hairpin bends and then alongside the walled grounds of a country house on your left. The road is joined by the B57, where you turn left to the memorial headland of **Noirmont★** (4.5mi 🎞⩎***P***3), shown opposite and described on page 33.

Return on the B57, passing roads on your left to Portelet Common (Short walk 2-2, with a splendid view over the bay) and L'Ouaisné (☕✕WC), where Walk 2 begins. Join the A13 and turn left. Stay on the main road only briefly until, at a fork, you drop down left on the B66 to **St Brelade's Bay★** (7mi ✝⛰⌂✕⊕☕WC). The lovely church is at the end of the road, just above the harbour. Behind the church, take the road signposted to Beau Port Bay and climb through more hairpin bends. You pass the road to **Beau Port★** (🎞⩎***P***2; photograph page 11) on your left: perhaps make a detour to look at this pretty, unspoiled cove .

Otherwise, come to a T-junction and turn left on the B83 to **La Corbière★** (9mi 🎞⛰✕⩎WC***P***4; Walk 4), one

Walk 3 and Picnic 3: World War II weaponry at Noirmont, the headland memorial to Jersey's war dead. St Helier is in the distance. See also photograph page 34.

of the best-known sights in Jersey, and really spectacular if you catch it at sunset or when the sea is running high over the rocks in a sou'west gale! Continue on the B44, then turn left on the B35. You pass a signposted path to La Sergenté, the oldest tomb on the island (11mi **⋔**; Walk 4), with parking nearby. Now you're at the southern end of **St Ouen's Bay**, a glorious five-mile sweep of beach, much favoured by surfers. Continue north past the **nature reserve** on the right and the **Kempt Tower** on the left — a true Martello Tower, built in 1834 and named for one of Wellington's generals at Waterloo. There are picnic sites and bird hides in **La Mielle de Morville** (**P**5a) opposite, and occasional guided walks in the nature reserve: details from Jersey Tourism (01 534 448877) or the National Trust for Jersey (01 534 483193).

The unusual boat-shaped building on the sea wall is let out for self-catering holidays by Jersey Heritage. Near the Château Plaisir shopping complex (including Jersey Woollen Mills) is the **Channel Islands Military Museum**, housing German and Allied vehicles and memorabilia in a former Nazi bunker (**M**■). Opposite is **Jersey Pearl**, a spacious

La Grève de Lecq: part of the collection of horse-drawn vehicles (far left) and 'Prisoner in his cell' — one of the tableaux depicting army life. Walk 7 also visits these 19th-century barracks, owned by the National Trust for Jersey.

15

The Devil, to be seen (where else?) but at Devil's Hole (Walk 7)

emporium and restaurant.

At the end of this long, straight stretch of road, turn right; this is the B64. Very shortly turn sharp left onto the B35 and pass **Treasures of the Earth** (15.5mi) on your right, an exhibition of geological relics (📻WC).

This low-lying area is **L'Etacq★**, which terminates in the imposing rock formation of Le Grand Etacquerel; (16.5mi 📷). Walk 6 starts here with a steep climb to the heathland of Les Landes and visits the magnificent rock pinnacle shown on page 41 (**P**6). Climb the hill, then make a very sharp left turn at the top, on the B55 to **Grosnez★** (18mi ■📷), where Walk 7 starts and Walk 6 can also start. Head off on the track to the ruined 14th-century castle and enjoy the magnificent views (information boards describe its history). There is ample free parking.

Return to the B55 and bear left, then go left again to **Plémont★** (∩📷📻WC; Walk 7), where there is an excellent beach, a good beach café and caves to explore at low tide though parking (free) is very limited. Return again to the B55 and bear left. At about 20mi, turn sharp left on the B65 to **La Grève de Lecq★** (21mi ▲✕🎫📷📻MWC — plenty of free parking space here.) There's another fine beach and a 19th-century barracks owned by the National Trust for Jersey. This is worth a visit: there's an impressive collection of horse-drawn vehicles, an exhibition revealing the story of Grève de Lecq's past and its tourist attractions, a special exhibition devoted to Jersey's north coast, a gift shop and visitor centre and, of course, exhibits devoted to its military history. Walk 7 passes here, too.

Head out of La Grève de Lecq on the B40, then turn left on the B33 and left again on the C103. Pass La Mare Wine Estate and come to **Devil's Hole★** (24mi ∩📷 📻WC), where a steepish path leads from the parking area (free) down to a wild sea inlet, passing the impressive 10ft statue shown opposite.

Now return to the B33, then almost immediately turn

left onto the B26 to reach St Mary. Then turn left again onto the B53. Now look for — and follow — the signs to **Lion Park**★ (✕ ◪WC), home of Jersey Goldsmiths. Enjoy exploring acres of delightful gardens, nature trails and parkland, with wildlife including red squirrels and pink flamingos. There's also a large lake on which radio-controlled model ships are available for use and there are extensive and spectacular showrooms of jewellery and other gifts. Children can play on a giant slide, a climbing frame and other amusements. A pleasant surprise — admission is entirely free of charge. Refreshment is catered for by an excellent tearoom and café with a choice of indoor or outdoor tables. On leaving the park, return to the junction of the B26 with the B53, then turn left (i.e. south) onto the B26.

Continue down the valley, bearing left on the A11 at a fork. Just before the Victoria Hotel, on the right, there is a small car park near the mill pond. Stop here briefly and walk through a lovely bit of woodland to Le Moulin de Quetivel, a mill of 14th-century origin (see Walk 13). From the Victoria Hotel you could follow signs to **The Living Legend**★ (✕ ◪WC). Or turn right and follow the road to the turn-off (B89) for the **Jersey War Tunnels**★ (31mi ◪WC). Walk 13 (page 56) starts here, and takes in both attractions.

From the tunnels car park cross into Meadow Bank, instead of rejoining the road on which you approached. Turn left on the A10 at La Ville Emphrie and go through **St Lawrence** (33mi; Walk 12). Less than half a mile beyond the church, turn right into Chemin des Moulins (C119) and follow this road as it loops around to the right, to a T-junction. Turn right here on the C118, to go down Waterworks Valley (**P**12). This road winds delightfully between wooded slopes, reservoirs and meadows. You reach the A1 at **Millbrook**, where a left turn will take you back to **St Helier** (36mi).

Lion Park (see above)

Car tour 2: THE EAST END

St Helier • Sion • Pallot Steam Museum • (Bouley Bay) • Jersey's zoo • Rozel • St Catherine's Bay • Mont Orgueil • La Hougue Bie • La Rocque • Green Island • St Helier

24mi/38km; about 2 hours' driving plus time for visits en route

On route: ⊟ at St Catherine's Bay, La Hougue Bie; Picnics (see pages 9-11): (7b), 9, 11a, 11b, 14, 15; Walks 7, 9, 10, 11, 14, 15

All roads are excellent but narrow in places, with sharp bends (especially near Rozel. Stick to the 40mph speed limit.

Leave St Helier by heading out on the Esplanade following the signs for St Aubin, but get in the right-hand lane by the time you approach the end of the Esplanade. Go around the roundabout, following signs for the A9: this is the road you want. It follows the curve of the park (which is on your left) then directs you onto the ring road by turning right into Cheapside. Follow the ring road left into Elizabeth Place and continue along Rouge Bouillon. Watch the signs and take the A9 on the left from the roundabout at the Queen's Road junction.

You leave the town behind as you take the Grand Route de St Jean and come to **Sion** (3mi), where there is an old Methodist Chapel (✝ 1880) built like a temple. It is enormous in relation to the size of the village. Past the chapel, on the right, is Macpela Cemetery, where European exiles who made Jersey their home in the mid-19th century were buried.

About a quarter of a mile past the chapel, turn right into Rue de Bechet, looking out for the signs to the fascinating **Pallot Steam Museum★**. This is an extensive, if informal collection assembled over several years by Mr Pallot, a local engineer. There are steam and diesel railway engines, rolling stock and a few hundred yards of full standard gauge railway track laid out in a circuit in the field behind the museum where, if you choose the right time to visit, you can ride in a train like the one shown below. In any case, at least one item is operating under steam at all times the museum is open. There are

A 1931 steam locomotive hauling Victorian coaches on the full-size standard gauge railway at the Pallot Steam Museum

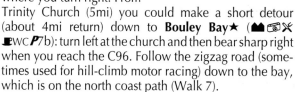

One of the gorillas from the famous colony at Jersey's zoo

traction engines, rare old farm machines and other machines of all kinds … there's even an organ room! Truly a surprising sight, tucked away in the heart of the island.

Leave the museum on a minor road opposite the entrance, to join the B51, where you turn right. From Trinity Church (5mi) you could make a short detour (about 4mi return) down to **Bouley Bay★** (🏔🍴✖ ⚓WC **P**7b): turn left at the church and then bear sharp right when you reach the C96. Follow the zigzag road (sometimes used for hill-climb motor racing) down to the bay, which is on the north coast path (Walk 7).

The main drive continues straight ahead from Trinity Church, on the B31. At 6mi come to the famous Durrell Wildlife Conservation Trust (**Jersey's zoo★**), which does splendid work in breeding rare species and is noted for its gorilla colony. This is a must, though it's probably best to reserve at least half a day for your visit here as admission is quite expensive and there is much to see.

After passing the zoo entrance, turn left on the C93, which is a pleasant run above the coastal path along to **Rozel★** (9mi 🏔✖🍴⚓WC). Rozel, where Walk 7 ends, is an attractive little fishing village with a hotel, restaurant, pub and café — possibly ideal for an away-from-it-all holiday. To join circular Walk 9 here at Rozel, see map page 47 and notes page 48.

Climb out of Rozel on the B38 and look out for the B91 on the left. Reach a minor crossroads (on the route of both Walk 9 and Walk 10) and bear right past an antique dealer's. Beyond Les Mares and Le Villot, you join the B29. Turn left. You pass La Mare slipway, where Walk 9 begins (**P**9).

Then come to **St Catherine's Bay★** and Breakwater (12mi 🍴🍽⚓WC), where Walks 10 and 11 begin. There is plenty of free parking space here, so why not stretch your legs on the breakwater or, for more variety of scene, try short circular Walk 10.

From St Catherine's Bay return on the B29, first coming

This pleasant spot near the entrance to Rozel woods (Picnic 9 and Walk 9) is only a few minutes' walk from a convenient parking spot at La Mare slipway.

to **Archirondel** (⬛**P**1a with ⌐) and then **Anne Port** (WC**P**1b with ⌐). Take a sharp left to head into **Gorey** ('Gouray' on the large-scale walking map; 14mi ✝⬛⬛▲ ✕⬛⊕⬛WC) and park by the harbour. Walk up to **Mont Orgueil Castle★** (⬛📷); the magnificent view from here is shown on pages 12-13. Walk 11 (from St Catherine's) ends here. From either Anne Port or Gorey you could make an interesting diversion (signposted) to the **Dolmen de Faldouët** (⬛). See Walk 11 and map page 47.

From Gorey harbour follow signs to St Martin. Half a mile along, fork left on the B28. Short walk 14 starts at St Saviour's Hospital (15mi), at the northern end of the **Queen's Valley Reservoir** (**P**4, photograph page 59). Continue to **La Hougue Bie★** (16mi ✝⬛⌐ **P**15), where Walk 15 begins (see details page 60).

Leaving La Hougue Bie, head back the way you came. Pass the B46 off right, but bear right on the

You'll encounter quiet roads like this one on this tour. Show consideration for horse riders and drive slowly, especially in the narrow lanes.

B37, past La Hougue Grange on your left. The road bends sharp left. Follow it until you can turn sharp left to the southern end of the Queen's Valley Reservoir (this is another place where you could park and do circular Short walk 14). Keep on this narrow road to **Jersey Pottery★** (17.5mi ✕WC) entry free, where you can see the whole manufacturing process — even make your own pots.

From the pottery head right to the A3, and there bear right again, to follow the coast. Soon the coast road becomes the A4 (the A3 cuts inland and would take you to St Helier via Grouville Church and Georgetown). The A4 gives you a chance to look at more of the coast; the seaward views are quite amazing at low tide, when the sea can recede more than two miles, revealing treacherous reefs. Your return to St Helier will be via **La Rocque**, **Le Hocq**, and **Le Croc** (honest: look at the map!), each of which has some parking space, permitting a break of journey for a brief look round.

As you near St Helier, you have a choice of routes, either via the road tunnel (turn right when you see the appropriate signs) or staying on the coast road past the open-air pool at Havre des Pas, eventually turning right into Pier Road. You pass the **Jersey Museum★** on the left, before turning left to arrive back at Liberation Square and the Maritime Museum (24mi).

Walking

The walks in this book are designed to take you to the loveliest parts of Jersey on the best footpaths.

Beginners: You can do most of the walks without problems, but the less nimble might find some stretches of the north coast path too steep for their liking.

Experienced walkers: All walks should be within your capability, including the north coast. This could be achieved in a day, but I would recommend making at least two days of it, to enjoy its sights fully.

All walkers: Please follow routes as described in the notes, especially where they are off-road. If at any stage you are uncertain of the way forward, go back to your last 'sure' point and start again. Do *not* try to continue a walk which for some reason has become impassable. And *I cannot emphasise too strongly* the need for caution when exploring Jersey's beaches at low tide. *Be absolutely sure of the tide times (check the local paper, or buy the tide tables at one of the shops) and always allow plenty of time to reach a safe point.*

W here to stay

Except perhaps during July and August, accommodation should never pose a problem: Jersey has an excellent range of registered hotels and guest houses (inspected and graded annually by Jersey Tourism). The Tourism office produces an excellent brochure giving details of all these premises (as well as camping sites) and operates a room-finder service (tel: 01 534 448888). Rather less self-catering accommodation is available, so if you wish to reserve an apartment, it is advisable to make your booking early in the year.

While most people stay around **St Helier**, you may prefer **St Aubin** or **St Brelade's Bay** to the west or **Gorey** in the east. Both are charming centres, with good public transport links to St Helier. There are also some pleasant small hotels and guest houses along the north coast and deep inland in the countryside.

W eather

Jersey has a summer average of 8 sunny hours a day (among the best in the British Isles), and rainfall averages 33-39 inches (80-100 cm) a year. May, June and July are generally considered the best months for a visit. August is warm, but can be thundery. March and April are often dry and sunny, and Jersey has known many an 'Indian summer' in September and October.

What to take

For much of the country walking in this book, you will need little special equipment. Some walkers find trainers adequate, but I will always recommend light-weight boots which cope with almost any conditions underfoot, which in Jersey might include long wet grass, rock pools, sand dunes, muddy tracks and tarmac roads ... all on the same walk! Below is a checklist of items you might find useful, depending on the season, the weather, and the part of the island covered by your walk:

long-sleeved shirt and long trousers	binoculars and camera
waterproof trousers and anorak	small rucksack
spare jumper, extra socks	sunhat, suncream, sunglasses
groundsheet (picnic sit-upon)	bus timetable
telephone numbers of taxi operators	mobile phone
whistle (if you get stuck or lost)	first aid kit

A country code for walkers and motorists

The experienced rambler is used to following a 'country code', but the tourist who rarely ventures into the countryside may unwittingly cause damage or harm animals. Be aware of the following when walking:

- **Do not light fires** except at official barbecue sites. Never allow youngsters to play with matches, and never throw cigarette ends away. Fires are a very real hazard on headlands during dry summers and are difficult to deal with because of inaccessibility.
- **Keep dogs under proper control**, and **fasten all gates after you**.
- **Keep to paths** across farmland and avoid damage to fences, hedges and walls.
- **Leave no litter**: take it away or put it in a litter bin.
- **Protect wild and cultivated plants**, and never walk over cultivated land.
- **Go carefully** on narrow country roads, and don't block them by parking carelessly.
- **Respect the countryside** and the country way of life.
- The bird life of Jersey's coastal region is very impor-tant. **Do not disturb or annoy the birds**, especially during the nesting season (spring).

Below are some other points, particularly directed to

walkers planning a lengthy ramble in any of the more remote locations:

- **Do not walk alone**, and *always* tell a responsible person where you are going and what time you expect to return. If you walk in a group, and someone is injured, others can seek help, and there will be no need for **panic in an emergency**.
- **Do not overestimate your speed**; your pace will depend on the slowest walker in the group.
- **If a walk becomes unsafe**, do not press ahead.
- **Transport** at the end of a long walk is important
- It pays dividends to carry some **warm clothing** and **extra rations**, even in summer, in case you are delayed beyond sunset.

Waymarking and maps

While there are more **waymarks** and signposts for walkers now than there were when the first edition of this book was published, Jersey still does not have an extensive system of public footpaths. Privacy is a cherished commodity on the island, and attempts to create long-distance routes have been thwarted in the past, through landowners' reluctance to allow access.

Our **walking routes** have been overprinted on the 1:25,000 States of Jersey Ordnance Survey Map (the full map is readily available on the island from stationers and bookshops). However, our extracts cover the areas most visited by walkers, including much of the island's coast. Where different spellings exist for place names, we have generally used the spellings on this map, to avoid confusion. Following is a **key to the symbols** on the walking maps.

B 46 — main road	P — car park (public)	♦/♦ church/chapel (with tower or spire)
C 109 — secondary road	P — car park (private)	+ church/chapel (without tower or spire)
— other roads, tracks or drives	⛟ suggested car park for walk or picnic	CH club house
— footpaths	✗⛩ picnic sites	F Sta fire station
		FB footbridge
→ route of the main walk and direction	☀ major viewpoints	F fountain
	☺ best views on walk	G garage
		Liby library
→ alternative route described in text	♦ ☎ WC, telephones	MS milestone
		Mus museum
walk recommended by Jersey Tourism	quarry	PH pub
		PO post office
🚌 bus terminus	■ castle, fort, tower	Sch school
	⬥ prehistoric site	T telephone
🚌 suggested bus stop for walk or picnic	Castle other antiquity	Twr tower
	∩ caves	TH town hall

Walk 1: ST HELIER HERITAGE

Distance: up to 3mi/5km; 1h30min-2h

Grade: very easy

You will need: stout shoes, credit card (optional!)

How to get there: 🚌 or 🚗 to Pier Road (paycard required) [18].

The history of Jersey and its main town of St Helier is vivid and sometimes bloody. Jersey Tourism [1 on the plan; tel: 01534 448877] and the Jersey Museum are good places to start learning about the island.

Start out from **Liberation Square**: cross the open area to the **Jersey Museum** [3], with its distinctive clock face. Inside you will find paintings, furniture, maritime displays and Victoriana. Along with other relics, including her travelling case, there are two portraits of Jersey's famous actress daughter, Lillie Langtry, one of which is by Jerseyman Sir John Everett Millais. The Société Jersiaise (Jersey Society) next door has an excellent bookshop and library, and welcomes serious enquiries.

Jersey Tourism
Bus Station
Jersey Museum
Parish Church
States Assembly
Royal Court
Indoor Market
Methodist Chapel
Jubilee Cross
Don Memorial
Hospital
Opera House
to Elizabeth Castle
Maritime Museum
Outdoor Pool
Jardins de la Mer and Waterfront
Fort Regent
Pier Rd Car Park
Post Office
Ferry Terminal
Town Hall
Police Station

St Helier

Take steps from their office to Pier road and walk down the hill to Mulcaster Street, then cross into Bond Street, to reach the west gate of **St Helier Parish Churchyard** [4]. According to legend, Helier was a 6th-century missionary who was murdered by pirates using axes, hence the symbolic crossed axes chosen as the emblem of the parish. The small chapel built on the rock where he lived near Elizabeth Castle became a place of pilgrimage known as the Hermitage. Walk through the churchyard (and indeed the church) and come to Church Street, once known as La Rue Trousse Cotillon or 'the street of raised petticoats' ... raised just enough for the ladies to cross what was once a filthy, muddy access to the Market Place, now known as **Royal Square**, which you are about to enter.

On the right are the **States' Assembly** [5; Jersey's parliament] and **Royal Court House** [6]. On the left there is an unusual wall-mounted sundial, and at the far end stands an imposing gilded statue of George II. In the far corner is the Peirson Inn (misspelled in the pub windows). It dates from 1749 but was named after Captain Peirson, who led a stirring victory over the marauding French on 6th January 1781, a day when Royal Square ran deep with blood. This last serious attempt by the French to capture Jersey is recorded in a painting in the Tate Gallery, London, a copy of which hangs in the Royal Court. Just opposite the Peirson, note a fire insurance company mark on the wall of a jeweller's shop. In the early days of fire-fighting, your fire would only be put out if you had paid the premiums beforehand. No plaque? Well, then you had a conflagration, sir.

Leave the square near the pub, then turn right to reach the pedestrianised shopping zone of King Street/Queen Street. Turn right, then go left down Halkett Street, which brings you into Beresford Street where you should make a point of visiting the fish market — a feast for the eyes! Coming out, cross the street to visit the main **Central Market** [7], which is a colourful melange of flowers, fruit, and vegetables surrounding a café and fountain.

There are many eateries around the market area: you can try a 'Jersey Wonder' from a bakery or sample Jersey ice cream or genuine Jersey products such as apple brandy or black butter (made from apples, not milk). And there are Italian, Portuguese, oriental, French and other restaurants to suit every taste. Leaving the market, come out into Halkett Place. Turn right and continue almost to the end of Halkett Place (crossing Burrard Street), to see the colourful façade of the **Methodist Chapel** [8] facing you at the end of the street. If you are a collector, you may like to know that you are now in a part of St Helier that is crammed with small shops and galleries, selling bric-a-brac, craft and off-beat items. From here walk back through Halkett Place to regain Queen Street.

Once back at Queen Street, turn right and walk along King Street shopping precinct to Charing Cross. Here you find a **granite cross** [9] commemorating the Queen's Jubilee in 1977. Note its depiction of twelve aspects of Jersey life, from St Helier's Hermitage to a sailing ship, from a milk can to an ormer (the island's native shellfish delicacy). The surrounding flower bed is edged with granite blocks taken from every quarry on the island and stone from the offshore reefs.

The indoor market in St Helier displays Jersey's produce at its finest. The central part of the market, ranged round a lovely ornamental fountain, includes a café.

Elizabeth Castle and its causeway.

As you bear right along York Street to the **Town Hall** [21], (where there is a superb collection of paintings to be seen in the Assembly Room), you will see a pillar with a sculpted toad on top. The toad (*crapaud* in French) is the nickname — rudely given by Guernseymen — to island-born men. The road ahead passes the island's Cenotaph and widens into the Parade, with a fine **statue of General Sir George Don** [10] in the gardens near All Saints Church. He was a famous early 19th century Lieutenant-Governor known as 'the roadmaker'.

Turn left into Gloucester Street, passing to the left of the **General Hospital** [11] and a nurses' home built on the site of the original Jersey prison (the present jail is on the coast east of La Corbière). On the left you'll see the **Opera House** [12], a fine Edwardian theatre restored in 2001 — definitely worth a visit.

Gloucester Street leads to the Esplanade, where you could turn right to get to the **causeway** [13] to Elizabeth Castle (Picnic 1), which starts almost opposite the Grand Hotel, but you might prefer to save this for a whole morning or afternoon. If you *do* walk over, be sure of the tides. (You can also make the trip in an amphibious 'ferry'. The Jersey Tourism office will tell you about the castle, which is well worth an excursion.)

Now cross the Esplanade safely at one of the pedestrian crossings with lights, to visit **Les Jardins de la Mer** [[16] — beside La Frégate café, which is shaped like an upside-down boat. This seaside park has pebbled and paved walkways with a wonderful 'dolphin' fountain where children can play in a maze of water jets. Nearby is the relatively new **Waterfront** development, with cafés and restaurants, a nightclub, gymnasium, apartments and a leisure pool with wave machine and beach area. The reclaimed land on which it is sited links the old harbours and modern ferry terminal via walkways through to **Albert Pier** and the lifeboat station. Walk on to the **Maritime Museum** [14] on New North Quay, from where you cross back to **Liberation Square** — ending the walk after **1h30min** to **2h**, depending on how long you've spent looking at the sights.

Walk 2: ST BRELADE • BEAU PORT • LA LANDE DU OUEST • CORBIERE

See also photograph page 11

Distance: 7.5mi/12km; 3h40min

Grade: easy to moderate; there are some steep ascents/descents with steps on the paths near Beau Port and around Corbière

You will need: comfortable shoes and long trousers (parts of the path may be overgrown with gorse). Binoculars could be useful.

How to get there and return: 🚌 12 to St Brelade's Bay and join the walk at St Brelade's Church, or 🚗 to L'Ouaisné car park (free).

Short walk: L'Ouaisné — Beau Port — L'Ouaisné (4.5mi/7km; 1h40min; easy). Access as main walk. Follow the main walk as far as the headland overlooking Beau Port and return the same way.

Alternative walk: link the walk with Walk 3 via the steeply stepped stony path that climbs up from **L'Ouaisné** beach to **Portelet Common**.

Strollers' corner (as I call it) is perfect for early morning or evening rambles, with some stunning scenery between Beau Port and Corbière.

Starting at **L'Ouaisné** (pronounced 'Waynay') car park, head across the sands (tide permitting) or go along the edge of the common on the sea wall and up over **Le Grouin** point to **St Brelade's Church (25min)** at the far end of the bay, by the harbour. Parts of the church are Norman; the adjacent fishermen's chapel is thought to be of 12th-century origin. (In the southeast corner of the churchyard is the island's shortest sanctuary path (*perquage;* unfortunately gated and locked) — along which criminals could escape justice centuries ago, if they vowed never to return. Nearby is a viewpoint.)

Leave the churchyard by turning left out of the lych-gate (opposite a sign for 'LE BEAU PORT'). Go up the path under trees on your right, to a road. Turn left for 200 yards/metres, then take signposted steps up the hillside and follow the ongoing path to **Beauport**. This is a quiet, unspoiled location with a very pretty beach (**45min**; Picnic 2; photograph page 11).

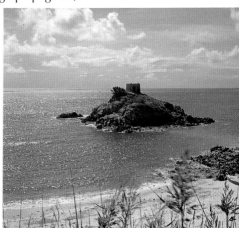

L'Ile au Guerdain in Portelet Bay once held the tomb of Philippe Janvrin, a sailor. He died from the plague in 1721, on a ship returning from France, and was initially buried here to minimise the risk of islanders contracting the disease.

Facing the sea, the path continues from the far right-hand corner of the car park. Take the right fork after some 100 yards/metres. The path twists through patches of gorse, bracken and brambles and at times can be overgrown. At the stone marked 'LA GROSSE TETE' and 'LE CREUX', bear right; after a few steps you will see another stone confirming you are on the coastal path. The next bit of the path is steep and with lots of steps.

When you reach the wall of a bungalow named 'Signal Point', turn right and walk a short distance to arrive at the perimeter fence of the island's **prison (1h10min)**. Here turn left on a road, then continue on the road as it turns right. Almost immediately you'll see the path (signposted) on your left — it passes a **weather radar station**. (Do *not* take the path to the left of the gateway of 'Maison Signaux'.) Now carry on across the exposed, often breezy, common of **La Lande du Ouest**.

Eventually pass two houses on your left, then drop down below the **desalination works** built on the site of an old quarry **(1h30min)**. The path runs on the seaward side of the works, then upwards beside an inclined plane railway track, now marked by wooden posts. Turn left as you reach the top and carry on along the cliff path. Soon you descend steep steps to a boulder-strewn beach. (A short detour on a path at the foot of the cliffs will take you to the mouth of a cave.) Then more steps take you up to another headland. In a few minutes you will see **Corbière and its lighthouse**, which you can visit at low tide.

When you reach the nearby bus stop (**1h50min**) you have the option of returning to St Brelade or back to St Helier by bus 12, shortening the walk by some 2mi/3km. (To extend the walk, perhaps link up with Walk 4.) Otherwise, retrace your steps to L'Ouaisné, using the sands or the promenade when you reach St Brelade, depending on the tide. At the end of the promenade, climb the steps to Le Grouin and ascend the hill either directly or via a gentler path to the right. Then follow a path down to the eastern half of the bay. It crosses private land, but walkers are welcome if they keep to the path. It passes an old tower and leads back to **L'Ouaisné** (**3h40min**).

Walk 3: NOIRMONT AND PORTELET BAY

See map pages 30-31; see also photograph page 15

Distance: 3mi/5km; 1h15min. (An optional extension to Portelet Beach adds at least 1mi/1.5km; 30-40min.)

Grade: easy, but the optional extension involves a fairly steep path and many steps to the beach at Portelet Bay, and a corresponding ascent — 200ft/60m.

You will need: comfortable shoes or trainers

How to get there and return: 🚌 12a to the Portelet terminus (Old Portelet Inn) or 🚗 to the Portelet car park (free). Return the same way.

Alternative walk: St Aubin — Noirmont — St Aubin (5mi/8km; 2h30min; grade as above). 🚌 9, 12, 12a, 15 or 🚗 to St Aubin harbour (paycard required). Walk south along the harbour, then climb a narrow road, to join the walk described below at the crossroads north of Le Manoir de Noir Mont (picking up the 'Foot and bridle path' mentioned in paragraph 2 on page 33). Return the same way.

This is a fairly short circular walk, although if you take in the optional visit to Portelet Beach, you'll need stamina for the stiff climb back up the 'never-ending' steps. (You can, however, enjoy some fine views of St Aubin's Bay and Portelet Bay without descending to the beach.) After your walk — or before descending to the beach — the Old Portelet Inn is an ideal place to take on some sustaining refreshment.

With the **Old Portelet Inn** on your right, and the car park/bus terminus behind you, **start the walk** by taking the narrow road that runs along the front of the pub. It shortly passes a riding stable (also on your right), and just a couple of minutes from the pub you come to a junction with a block of apartments in view.

Turn right here, pass the apartments (now on your left), and continue to a T-junction with the Portelet Hotel just visible across the road, to your left. Turn left here and walk the short distance to **Portelet Common (15min)**, for some stunning views over the bays of St Brelade and Ouaisné. This area, part of the National Trust for Jersey, is golden with gorse and purple with heather in the summer months. Take care — there are sheer drops around the old guard house and also over an old quarry face where a path comes up from Ouaisné. Make a circuit of the common (enjoying some excellent views of Portelet Bay) and, if you wish, walk through the gateway to enjoy the walk to **Le Fret** point. Maybe you'll be spending about 20 minutes or so on the common, leaving it at about **35min**.

Return to the road, pass the **Portelet Hotel** on your left and continue until you reach another junction where a road climbs uphill from the left. Here you turn right. Be careful: the road is narrow, and there can be a fair amount of traffic (**45min**).

Shortly, you'll come to a crossroads. Here you leave the road and take the pathway through a wooded area. look for it on the other side of the junction, to the right. The path briefly passes through the woods, then you'll find yourself in semi-moorland, with huge clumps of gorse and broom, a glorious blaze of gold with a heady fragrance, especially in May and June. Avoid the new bridleway here; the *main path has a netting fence on the left* which marks the boundary of the grounds of Le Manoir de Noir Mont (private property, not open to the public). On your right you'll see many meandering side-paths along which you can wander if you are so inclined; they all eventually lead back to the main path, which you can recognise by the adjacent fencing.

A few minutes' walking will bring you to more open land, and you will see your destination in the distance. As you approach Noirmont car park, one of the preserved gun emplacements comes into view and, momentarily, you can visualise what the heavily-defended coast of the island looked like during the Second World War. **Noirmont** (the 'black hill'; Picnic 3) is a headland at the western end of St Aubin's Bay and is so named because it looms dark in certain conditions when viewed from St Helier.

You'll reach two German guns (**55min**), stark symbols of Jersey's dark days of Occupation. Even more stark is the German bunker built into the headland (see the photograph overleaf), maintained as a museum by the Channel Islands Occupation Society. It is open for viewing occasionally during the summer but if you want to visit it, do check opening times with Jersey Tourism (tel: 01 534 448877) because as each year passes, there seem to be a steadily decreasing number of the band of enthusiasts needed to keep it open.

Spend a few more minutes in reflection while looking round the relics. From the main car park, walk back along the road which

Broom and gorse weave paths of gold on the way back to Noirmont.

Some of the relics of the Occupation at Noirmont (see also photograph page 15).

vehicles use to reach the headland. After some 300 yards/metres turn left onto a footpath which will take you across to a **viewpoint** (**1h05min**) from which you can see Portelet Bay with L' Ile au Guerdain as its focal point.

Retrace your steps a short distance; then, instead of continuing on the path back to the car park, take a path which forks left. In a couple of minutes, fork left again. This path will take you along the cliff-top to the Portelet car park and bus terminus and, of course, the **Old Portelet Inn** (**1h15min**).

If you want to extend the walk to Portelet Beach, look for a path on the seaward side, near the car park/bus terminus — it's signposted to **Portelet Bay** and you'll probably see a notice warning that there are no toilets on the beach. This diversion will take a minimum of half an hour. The path soon becomes steps. Once on the beach — depending on the state of the tide — you could also climb to the top of **L'Ile au Guerdain** and explore the tower marking the original site of Janvrin's tomb. (You'll see another path up from the beach a short distance to the right from the one by which you descended, but it's inadvisable to attempt returning by this path because although it would take you up to the top road, it passes through an area which is private property.)

By the time you've struggled back up the steps, you'll be more than ready to call in at the Old Portelet Inn — for liquid or more sustaining refreshments!

Walk 4: THE CORBIERE WALK

See map pages 30-31; see also photographs pages 5, 10, 17 and cover
Distance: 8mi/13km; 3h30min   Grade: easy
You will need: stout shoes, sunhat, water in hot weather, binoculars
How to get there and return: 🚌 9, 12, 12a, 15 or 🚌 to St Aubin harbour (paycard required); return the same way.

It's a long time since a steam railway operated from St Helier via St Aubin, along the wide bay, to La Corbière lighthouse, one of Jersey's most visited landmarks. The old route makes an excellent, easy walk.

I have varied the route from the signposted walk (extending the total distance slightly), to give you much finer views and a close look at a sand-dune environment, as well as some prehistoric standing stones. Birdwatchers could find this route a happy twitching-ground, for woodpecker and warbler, wader and finch.

At **St Aubin harbour**, where the road turns inland, **the start** of the **Corbière Walk** is well indicated at the entrance to a short tunnel. Follow the walk for about 2mi/3km through pleasant woodland (crossing two roads), until **Les Quennevais School** is on your left (**50min**). On the right are its playing fields and beyond, the edge of **La Moye golf course**. Between them is a path: follow it a little way, under pine trees. You emerge with the playing fields on the right and sandy golf links on the left. Ahead is a good view of Jersey airport. Carry on for a few minutes, then turn left across the dunes (near a stile). There is no clear path: just choose the easiest way. This area is known as **Les Blanches Banques** and is of great interest to botanists who cherish its rare wild orchids and variety of grasses. It's part of the three-mile stretch of dunes known as **Les Mielles**. The dunes contain over 400 plant species including 15 rare species.

Ahead is the magnificent sweep of **St Ouen's Bay** (pronounced One's), and you will see Rocco Tower to the south of it. Look over the lower sandy plain towards the tower, and you should spot a **standing stone** (menhir) which is your next landfall. Head down from the upper dune system along the easiest route you can find and inspect the stone (with a 'sister' stone and a small burial chamber nearby). Some of Jersey's many prehistoric sites are believed to have been associated with primitive forms of worship.

La Corbière lighthouse now lies south. Head towards it, across the lower dune area. You make easy progress now. Your first target is a car park with steps leading out

35

In the early 1900s passengers alight from a train at the Corbière terminus of the railway line from St Helier.

of it past an old German bunker on the right. You will then look over a second car park: drop down to it and, at the far end, cross the road. Follow the roadside path until you reach a sharp left-hand bend. Here the main path curves right, round the base of a cliff, but you can first climb to the top of the cliff to see **La Sergenté**, the oldest tomb on the island (3700 BC). It's a private path with permitted access. The lower path (also private with permitted access) brings you round to **Le Petit Port** (**1h40min**), a pretty bay offering shelter to a wide variety of birds, especially waders and warblers.

From here it's another 15-20 minutes along the road to **La Corbière** (Picnic 4) — spectacular in a winter southwesterly storm. If the tide is out, you can walk across the causeway to the lighthouse (see cover photograph), but watch you don't get caught by the incoming tide! (A siren sounds when the causeway is about to be covered by the tide.)

From the terminus near La Corbière you can catch bus 12, timetable permitting. The main walk continues back to St Aubin: look out for a path on the left, as you walk up the road (it's opposite the toilets and sign-posted 'CORBIERE WALK'). The path will bring you to the old station shown below, now 'enhanced' by a glazed extension. Facing the station (on the far side of the track), look out for the **Table des Marthes**. Popular myth has it that the great block of red granite is part of a prehistoric tomb and that, a hundred years ago, a contract signed on this stone was as binding as one made legally. To end the walk, just follow the track all the way back to **St Aubin** (**3h30min**).

Today the station is the starting (or end) point for walks, not trains. The Table des Marthes is just visible.

Walk 5: LE VAL DE LA MARE

Distance: 5.25mi/8.5km; 3h

Grade: moderate; there are a few steep (though short) sections.

You will need: stout shoes, long trousers, sunhat, water in hot weather

How to get there and return: 🚌 9 (alight at New Road) or 🚗 to the Val de la Mare car park on the A12 (free); return the same way.

Short walk: Circuit of the Val de la Mare Reservoir (2.75mi/4.5km; 1h15min; easy). Access as above. Follow the main walk for 30min. Then climb up the other side of the valley and continue to skirt the reservoir. You will cross a causeway and enjoy fine views to St Ouen's Bay (Picnic 5b). On reaching your outgoing path, follow it back to the bus stop/car park.

This is the most varied of our walks, taking in a lovely reservoir circuit, a section of country park, and a Neolithic burial chamber. It will not seriously challenge experienced walkers, but has one or two steep sections.

Start the walk at the bus stop/car park on the A12: take the waymarked path to the **Val de la Mare Reservoir** (built in the 1960s; **15min**). Bear left here, and follow the waterside path round to the 100ft/30m-high dam and from there descend to the valley floor at the **foot of the dam** (**30min**). *Those doing the Short walk continue up the other side of the valley, to circle the reservoir.*

Follow the reservoir road seawards to reach Rue de la Mare. Here turn right for about 1mi/1.25km, to the junction with Mont Matthieu (a road) on your right. (Those interested in wartime relics might wish to make a short detour some 400yards/metres up this road, to the neglected remains of one of a very few wartime bunkers bearing original German Bauhaus style lettering cast in concrete: GESTEINSBOHR KOMP 77. The bunker is on the right. Allow half an hour extra for this detour, marked in dashed green lines on the map.)

Not far beyond the Mont Matthieu turning, go up a wide unsurfaced sandy track on the right (**1h**) — *not* the surfaced track shortly after, which leads to houses. After some 200 yards/metres come to a junction of paths with a waymark bearing the traditional acorn symbol. Here turn left — it was originally an old donkey trail dating from the time when *vraic* (seaweed) was used by farmers as a fertiliser. The path veers right and goes uphill. You'll pass by a pond on your right (it could be hidden behind bushes, depending on the time of year) and arrive at a house named La Ville au Bas (**1h20min**).

Turn left here and follow a wider, but still rough track for a short distance, until you arrive at a junction. Ignore a bridle path coming up from the left at 45° and make a 90° left turn to follow the waymarked route. It soon loops round and descends along the edge of a field into a valley, **Les Vaux Cuissin** (named on a small plaque on the left). Beyond a sometimes overgrown section you cross a little wooden bridge over a stream, then rise up to more fine views. Soon there are glasshouses over to your right and a high privet hedge alongside you, as you reach a metalled road, Le Chemin des Monts. Turn left for about

Picnic 5b: Le Val de la Mare Reservoir, with St Ouen's Bay in the distance.

The path down to Les Vaux Cuissin. In the distance, fine views of St Ouen's Bay stretch from Corbière to Le Grand Etacquerel.

350 yards/metres, from where the **Dolmen des Monts Grantez** is accessible across a field on your left. It's one of the more substantial prehistoric graves on the island; uncovered in 1912, it yielded several 5000-year-old skeletons. The National Trust for Jersey owns this area, so you are free to wander down paths to **L'Etacq** and **St Ouen's Bay**.

Retrace your steps back to the road. Bear right and keep straight on past the house named Les Vaux Cuissin (where you came onto Le Chemin des Monts). When you come to a T-junction, turn right and keep walking until you come to a fork. There is a **derelict windmill** to the right of the right-hand fork. Take the left fork, a lane marked 'dead end', and follow it to **St Ouen's Church 2h10min**. (From here you could walk about half a mile east to St Ouen's Manor crossroads, to pick up bus 9.)

The main walk continues by turning right from the main door of the church. Then take the first left into La Rue de la Campagne, walking past fields still strip-farmed as in medieval times. At a road junction, turn right, then very soon bear left on a track signposted to the Val de la Mare Reservoir. Take the left fork in the track and, at a small car park, go through a gate and descend a narrow path to the edge of the reservoir.

Turn left to follow the path round this arm of the reservoir, cross a **causeway** and climb up to enjoy splendid views towards St Ouen's Bay, with the airport over to your left. There are seats here, and grassy slopes which make an excellent picnic spot (Picnic 5b). Fifteen minutes later you reach your outward route; follow it back to the **Val de la Mare** bus stop/car park (**3h**).

Walk 6: THE PINNACLE

See map of the north coast on the reverse of the touring map. You can of course easily link this walk with Walk 7 if you wish.

Distance: 3mi/5km; 1h30min

Grade: moderate

You will need: stout shoes, binoculars

How to get there and return: You can begin this walk at either Grosnez or L'Etacq. 🚌 8 or 🚗 to the free car park at Grosnez; 🚌 12a or 🚗 to the free car park just below the rock formation Le Grand Etacquerel (the L'Etacq bus terminus); return the same way.

Witchcraft and pagan rituals have made their mark on Jersey's history. While researching this book, I exercised my usual traveller's curiosity at most relevant sites, without being turned into a toad or even faintly discomfited. But there *is* something disturbing about this windswept cliff-top, with its Nazi detritus, and the claustrophobic amphitheatre. See what you think. For good measure there's Grosnez 'castle', the ruins of a 14th-century defence against the French who were demonstrably given to looting, pillaging, arson, rape, and murder on many a bloodthirsty 'away-day'.

So you tread on interesting soil. **Start out** at either Grosnez or Le Grand Etacquerel. From **Grosnez** just follow the cliff-top path south, towards a German observation tower. From **Le Grand Etacquerel** climb the steep road behind the car park, to pick up the signposted path to the top of the cliff; you pass some bunkers and many other wartime relics, some rusting away, others looking almost as when they were built.

The 200ft/60m-high Pinnacle rock, **Le Pinacle** (Picnic 6) looks benign enough on the approach (**30min** from

A carpet of thrift on a sunny day at Grosnez, but mist is rising from the sea, creating an air of mystery and menace around the castle ruins.

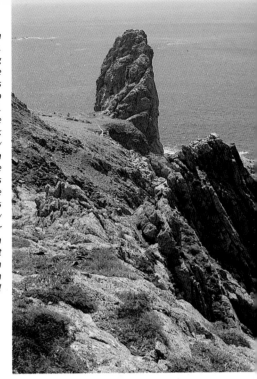

Picnic 6: from the distance, the towering mass of the Pinnacle does not look too formidable. However, the mighty stack will one day stand in isolation— the sea has undermined the cliff, which is now rapidly eroding. So, for your own safety, content yourself with admiring it from the cliff top!

Grosnez; **20min** from L'Etacq). Neolithic man once used the local rock and flints to fashion tools, including ceremonial axes. Earlier generations worshipped here, drawn, one imagines, by the face of the rock. (Come here in the early morning and see the almost human 'face' thrown into shadowy features by the sun as it rises above the rim of the cliff!) The natural amphitheatre must have swarmed with superstitious islanders who created the shrine at the base some 2,000 years ago. Today, this important archaeological site is suffering from erosion, so please do not descend from the cliff-top, because the cliff is crumbling, continually eroded by the sea.

There are splendid views along the whole coastline. After you have walked from Grosnez to Le Grand Etacquerel (or vice versa), you can vary your return route by taking the path slightly inland (see walking map on the reverse of the touring map). You will skirt **Les Landes racecourse**, where there are several meetings each summer, and pass a rifle range and an airfield for model aircraft. Whichever route you choose, you should be back at your transport in under **1h30min**.

Walk 7: THE NORTH COAST

See map on reverse of the touring map; see also photographs pages 14, 15, 16. You can link this walk with Walk 6 if you wish.

Distance: up to 15mi/24km; 7h30min (beginning at Grosnez). The walk is best done in two days, breaking at Bonne Nuit Bay.

Grade: quite strenuous in places

Equipment: stout shoes or light boots, tide table, binoculars, sun hat, picnic, water

How to get there and return: 🚌 bus links from and to St Helier at various points (see text for details of route numbers). At each point on the coast which you can reach by bus, the coastal path is very close to the bus stop. In many instances you will be able to see the path as you alight but, if you are in any doubt, ask at a kiosk or café and they will tell you where you can join the path. Or start by 🚌 and take a bus back to your parking place, but be aware that this will often involve taking a bus back to St Helier in order to get a bus or taxi from there back to where you left your car — on some routes this could take a couple of hours or more.

I have known masochistic walkers capable of devouring the whole of Jersey's coastline (about 40mi/65km) in a single trek. But they would have seen nothing, except the path ahead. You can 'do' the whole coast, seeing much more, but perhaps taking a week over it and gaining infinitely more pleasure from your exertions.

I have introduced you to some stretches of the coast in earlier walks, and other admirable rambles can be made without guidance — for instance between St Helier and St Aubin, Green Island and Gouray on the east coast, or on the flat but atmospheric route skirting St Ouen's Bay on the west coast.

But in this 'chapter' we'll look at Jersey's north coast, with its towering cliffs, sea caves accessible at low tide, wooded valleys, and stunning views over perilous reefs towards Guernsey and the other Channel Islands — and, at the eastern end, to France on a clear day.

You don't need a mass of directions to follow a coastal path: broadly speaking, if you move too far to one side you'll lose sight of the sea; too far the other way and you'll fall into it. Where the way ahead needs a pointer, you have one, as there are wooden signs and stone waymarks all the way along the coast.

So I will offer a guide to key stages on the 15mi/24km (approximately) of beautiful coast that stretches between Grosnez in the west (Walk 6) and Rozel in the east (Walk 9). It makes sense to me to divide this stretch into at least two days. Nowhere is it really difficult, and at several points you can escape by bus, take refreshment, or divert temporarily to other attractions.

The waterfall cave at Plémont

Begin the walk at **Grosnez**, (🚐 8 or 🚗). (If you use the bus, you'll have about a third of a mile to walk from the B55 before reaching Grosnez.) Heading east, the first port of call is **Plémont** (1.5mi/2.5km; **45min**; 🚐 7b, 8; with lovely views over La Grève au Lanchon beach. There's a waterfall cave *(no access)* running under the beach café, and you'll also see Needle Rock.

Next is **La Grève de Lecq** (4mi/6.5km; **2h**; 🚐 9), where the Moulin de Lecq pub has a waterwheel in the bar and you can visit the 19th-century barracks illustrated on pages 14 and 15 and described on page 16. There's also another excellent beach to explore and a choice of refreshment options. Climb the path indicated near the old barracks for about 0.6mi/1km, then detour round a shooting range (the route varies depending on whether firing — indicated by red flags — is in progress). Come to **Col de la Rocque**, a splendid headland viewpoint.

Shortly reach **Devil's Hole** (6mi/10km; **3h**; 🚐 7) and a decent pub — the Priory. You pass a huge statue of the Devil rising out of a pool as you take the path down to the cave (photograph page 16). There's a steepish flight of steps at the end of the path, a peculiar cave with a blow-hole through which the sea crashes and the views reward your exertions. In 2006 this area was given to the National Trust for Jersey.

Retrace your steps to the main path and continue along another headland, then descend into **La Vallée des Mouriers** and climb out again for more excellent views. To the north, a mile or two offshore, lie the perilous rocks of Paternoster Reef. Walk 8 also follows this stretch of path, which leads to a superb viewpoint at Sorel but then has to leave the coast to avoid Ronez Quarry. This diversion is well enough signposted. The path continues along the heights, following a road built by islanders during the occupation (a stone tablet opposite Les Fontaines pub records their efforts). Ahead you'll see the island's television transmitter, a slender 'Eiffel Tower'! When you reach the junction of the C101 with its

Millennium Cross, walk a short way inland to the fascinating 'Farmhouse' bar and restaurant, where there's a pub located in an interesting old building.

Back on the path, you pass a smaller quarry (**3h 50min**). From here you should be able to see kestrels, gulls, fulmar and the common shag perched on the offshore Cormorant Rock. Pass a one-time pub, now a private house (near Picnic 7a), and in ten minutes or so, come to **Fremont Point**, from where you overlook the beautiful double sweep of Bonne Nuit and Giffard bays with Belle Hougue Point in the distance. Descend to **Bonne Nuit** (9km/14.5km; **4h30min**; 🚐 4), an ideal place for a break, with a café tucked beneath the cliff — and a bus stop on the hill.

Opposite the bus stop is a steep hillside once grazed by sheep, now owned by the National Trust for Jersey; here you can enjoy spectacular views from a circular path. The coast path resumes its way east now, passing between buildings before dividing into a lower and upper path. Either way will suit you, but it goes without saying that the best views are from the higher path. Beyond the headland of **La Belle Hougue** the paths combine again, leading past **Le Petit Port** (don't blink or you'll miss it) and through a lovely and equally *petit* bit of woodland, to come to **Bouley Bay** (12mi/19km; **6h**; 🚐 4 from Trinity Church; Picnic 7b).

Once a smugglers' haunt, and known to motor sport enthusiasts for its hill climb, Bouley is a picturesque bay framed by volcanic cliffs. Its steeply-shelving beach has been judged the cleanest in the UK, and there are superb underwater diving facilities. You can also take a side-stroll here if you wish, up to **Le Jardin d'Olivet**, scene of

a battle with the French in the 16th century.

Continue from the Water's Edge Hotel to arrive at delightful **Rozel** (15mi/24km) **7h30min**; 🚐 3; Walk 9). Before boarding your bus enjoy some refreshments here; the 'Hungry Man' kiosk on the pier is justly famous for its home-made food.

The coastal path near Sorel (Walks 7 and 8)

Walk 8: SOREL AND LA VALLEE DES MOURIERS

See map on the reverse of the touring map; see photograph opposite

Distance: 2mi/3km; 1h

Grade: moderate; the cliff path is occasionally rough, and there are short stretches of gradient, sometimes with lengthy stretches of steps.

You will need: stout shoes

How to get there and return: 🚗 to Sorel (two free car parks)

Alternative walk: St John's Church — Sorel — coastal path — St John's Church (5mi/8km; 2h30min; grade as above). 🚌 5 to St John's Church. Follow the C101 and C100 to the viewpoint at Sorel, then continue the main walk, before returning to St John's.

This short circular walk takes in farm land, a peaceful wooded valley, and a stretch of cliff path with fine views and good picnic spots overlooking the sea.

Start out at **Sorel**, a breezy headland adjacent to the busy **Ronez granite quarry**. Walk a few hundred yards/ metres back along the road you followed to reach the viewpoint. When you reach the T-junction (with Sorel farm immediately facing you), turn right. Follow the road round the farm buildings (they will be on your left) and keep with it as it takes a right-hand turn. Now, stay on this road, passing one or two houses and occasional roads and paths joining from the left. Still on the same road, at **15min** pass a junction on your left with a 'Give way' sign and soon start going downhill.

Come to a junction where there is a turning off to the right, and soon after, another to the left; ignore them both. When you reach the bottom of the hill, you will find yourself at a small crossroads (**25min**). Here, turn right, taking the road that runs along the left-hand side of a stream, the start of which may be hidden by weeds and foliage.

Now you come to the best part of the walk. Your route descends through the **Vallée des Mouriers** towards the sea. When the road you are on bends left and sweeps uphill past a cottage on your left, take a track that forks away to the right directly opposite the cottage. Pass a small **reservoir** on your right (**35min**). Shortly before you reach the sea (there's no beach, just a rocky shelf), look to the right for the coastal path and join it (Walk 7 also follows this section).

From here on, it's just a matter of following the cliff path which, though narrow in parts, is not hazardous, provided that the ground is dry underfoot. Look out for the grazing herd of Manx Loaghtan sheep which assist with conservation management; fencing and stiles have been introduced to contain them. In **1h** the path brings you back to **Sorel**.

Walk 9: AROUND ST MARTIN AND ROZEL

See also photographs pages 2 and 20

Distance: 5mi/8km; 3h

Grade: moderate; after a rainy spell, the woodland paths can be muddy. The path between Rozel and Le Havre de Scez (via the Dolmen du Couperon) is also both stony and rather steep in short stretches.

You will need: stout shoes or walking boots

How to get there and return: 🚌 to the car park at St Catherine's Tower, south of the La Mare slipway (free but limited space).

This delightful inland walk takes you through woodland and along quiet country roads and paths flanked by carpets of wild flowers. It also visits the seaside village of Rozel and the Dolmen du Couperon.

From **St Catherine's Tower**, **start out** by turning left and walking up the road, away from the sea. When you reach the crossroads, bear right along the one-way road marked with a 'no entry' sign (for vehicles). Almost immediately, turn left on a track that leads to Rozel woods. This stony track first takes you past a small private fishing pond which began life as a German-built reservoir during the Occupation. It then leads into **Rozel Woods** (Picnic 9), across two lots of stepping stones and alongside a pretty stream. This is the habitat of birds like the great spotted woodpecker, also the red squirrel, the latter a rare creature now on the British mainland.

Follow the path for about **20min**, ignoring another path which joins it from the left (the old *perquage* or 'sanctuary path' from St Martin, down which in days gone by villains could legitimately flee the island if they promised never to come back!).

In less than 200 yards/metres, come to a T-junction of paths and go left. The path now climbs fairly steeply out of the woods. After another 400 yards/metres it becomes surfaced with tarmac and bends left, to take you past a farm on your left. As the farm buildings end, turn right. Walk along a lane which passes through farming land. You'll see on your left a huge multi-sided construction surmounted by a lot of mushroom-shaped domes. It looks like some enormous spacecraft that has just landed, but is part of the airport's navigational aids. You are now nearly at St Martin. A few minutes later, come out into Rue de Belin, where the Methodist Chapel is on your right. Pass the chapel and, within a few yards/metres emerge on the **main B38** (**40min**), where you turn right. (If you want to make a detour to the centre of the village of St Martin and the church, turn left instead, but make sure you return to take up the route from this spot.)

46

Le Moulin de Rozel

After ten minutes you cross a stream (though you may not be able to see any water for all the trees). Five minutes later reach a T-junction and go left. Soon you will have a good view of St Martin over to the left and, in another 200 yards/metres (near a postbox set in a wall), turn right into Rue du Moulin. You may be able to glimpse the tower shown here, the remains of one of Jersey's oldest windmills. Set in private grounds, it is a fine sight. Follow the road down through a narrow one-way system, dropping into **Rozel Valley** and turning right to reach **Rozel Bay** (**1h15min**).

Rozel is a lovely place to linger (the Hungry Man kiosk on Rozel pier is highly recommended for a snack) but, to continue the walk, climb the road, with superb views to your left over the harbour. At the top of the hill, look out on your left for a sign reading 'Public footpath to Le Scez' and take this path, which drops steeply with fine views over Rozel and the inlet of Le Douët de la Mer. The path twists and turns, drops and climbs, reaching **Le Couperon**, the prehistoric burial site shown opposite (just a few yards/metres to your left; **1h40min**). It is one of only two gallery graves in Jersey.

Continue downhill for a few yards/metres, to the end of Rue des Fontenelles. ('Rue' is rather an overstatement here and elsewhere in Jersey, where it describes even the most humble of paths.) At this point you will see a small car park and a path running off to the left of the main car park. This leads down to **Le Havre de Scez** (a sheltered anchorage rather than a harbour), where seaweed for fertilising the land was once collected. It's a pleasant and sometimes-deserted beach.

From here, you can see the sentry tower at the top of La Coupe, which you will visit a little later in the walk.

Go up the narrow road which twists and turns steeply uphill (it won a competition for the 'most scenic lane' in Jersey). Further up, a sign proclaims that the lovely area on your left is owned by the National Trust for Jersey. Unfortunately no paths run through it, and you must keep to the road.

The road soon veers quite sharply to the left and then levels out; take the first turning to the left. Follow this road down an increasing gradient until you reach **La Coupe** (**2h05min**), the promontory shown in the photograph below. There is access to a small beach down a path on the right.

Then climb back up the same road until you reach the T-junction. Turn left, following the road as it twists right, then left, as far as a crossroads. Go straight across and, not far beyond a riding centre on your right, turn into a road that forks back to the right (signposted 'Les Mares'). This passes between a few buildings and rapidly becomes a narrow farm track leading down to **Rozel Woods**. At the point where it changes to a hard surface and becomes walled on both sides, look across to the right for a fine view of Rozel Manor.

Continue down the track and come back to the junction where, earlier in the walk, you turned left to climb out of the woods and up to St Martin's. From here, turn left to retrace your steps past the stretch of water on your left, back to the car park at **St Catherine's Tower** (**3h**).

The Dolmen du Couperon. In the background, beyond Le Havre de Scez beach, is La Coupe, a small headland topped by a little tower.

Walk 10: A SHORT STROLL AROUND FLICQUET

See map page 47
Distance: 2mi/3km; 1h
Grade: easy, with just a couple of gradients (one steep and stony)
You will need: comfortable shoes or trainers
How to get there and return: 🚌 1b to St Catherine's Bay. 🚗 to St Catherine's Bay (ample free parking); return the same way.

Motorists often like to break their driving with a circular walk of a couple of miles. This one is ideal: it's often overlooked by those who park at St Catherine's Bay and, wanting a breather, simply walk to the end of the breakwater and back. The breakwater, a 850yd/800m-long granite structure, was built in the mid-1800s as the start of what was to have been a major harbour. However, before completion it was realised that it would be hopelessly silted up most of the time, so the Admiralty just finished its construction to save face.

Start out at **St Catherine's Bay** by walking back, along the loop road you've just used. In a matter of 200 yards/metres past the café and toilets, look out for a footpath on the right-hand side of the road. You will easily recognise it as there is a sign indicating 'FOOTPATH TO FLIQUET'. It's a steep and stony climb.

Soon you'll reach the bit of war-time history shown opposite: two sets of anti-tank barriers which were erected by the German Occupation forces. They consist of lengths of railway track embedded vertically in the pathway and they're a relic of Jersey's long defunct railways. As you near the top of the hill, look out for a waymarked post on your right and turn right into a field with many trees. (There is a seat from which you can enjoy the view; it also makes a pleasant picnic spot.) The grassy path through the field soon brings you out onto a secluded

You'll see these wartime relics in the first five minutes of your walk.

road. Here turn right and walk down the hill to the quiet little cove at **Flicquet**, with its ancient defence tower.

Pass the tower and continue along the road, which starts to climb gently. Soon you'll come to a pseudo-Spanish style house, a 20th-century folly built beside the road, on your left. The road takes a sharp hairpin bend to pass three sides of this unusual residence, then curves upwards past an attractive row of cottages set back on the right. The flowers surrounding these cottages can be spectacular if you pass by at the right time of the year.

Continue along the road, which is quiet and unlikely to have any traffic, apart from an occasional car seeking one of the very few parking spaces at tiny Flicquet. Pass a bungalow on your left; it appears to be built entirely from wooden tiles. At **25min** you reach a road junction: turn left. (Or, if you have time to spare and would like to extend your walk by half an hour, instead turn right, follow the road as it makes a sharp turn to the right and then to the left. Then, within a few yards/metres, take a road off to the right and follow it for about a third of a mile (500m), to the little headland of La Coupe shown on page 49. Retrace your steps to pick up the main walk again.)

Walk 9 also follows this short stretch of road, where the hedgerow is sometimes a mass of colourful flowers. Soon pass riding stables on the right and then a road off to Les Mares (where Walk 9 turns off to the right). In another 150 yards/metres, take the road on the left signposted to Flicquet. Pass minor turnings on both sides of the road until, after half a mile (800m) of gentle downhill gradient, the road takes a sharp turn to the left. Just at the point where it bends, take the track leading downhill to the right — it's the one you climbed at the start of the walk.

At the bottom of the hill, bear left beside the sea wall and follow the road. Within a couple of minutes you arrive at back **St Catherine's Bay** — ready, no doubt, for lunch or a cream tea (**1h**).

Walk 11: ST CATHERINE'S TO GOREY

See map page 47 and photograph pages 12-13

Distance: 3mi/5km; 1h15min

Grade: easy

You will need: stout shoes

How to get there and return: 🚐 1b to St Catherine's Bay. Return on 🚐 1 or 1b from Gorey to St Helier. Alternatively, 🚗 park at St Catherine's Bay (ample free parking) and after the walk do it in reverse back to your car at St Catherine's Bay (2h30min-3h30min).

Alternative walk: Flicquet — St Catherine's Bay — Gorey (5mi/8km; about 2h15min). Do Walk 10, then follow up with this walk.

Short though it is, this linear walk packs a variety of scenery into a few leisurely miles along the east coast. It starts at St Catherine's breakwater — a major harbour that never was; see page 50. It's about a mile out and back, if you wish to walk it first.

Start out by walking back along the main road you took to reach **St Catherine's Bay**, using the path that runs along the seaward side of the road. Pass **La Mare slipway** and **St Catherine's Tower** (Walk 9) and two picnic areas with barbecues (Picnic 11a). Then come to a second, 18th-century defence tower on a short breakwater at Archirondel. Immediately beyond it is **Archirondel Beach** (**35min**): not too crowded, it makes a fine picnic spot.

Leave the path here: go down to the beach and for a short distance walk on the pebbles. Then climb the third flight of steps you come to and follow a short path through a small field to the coast road (**50min**).

Turn right on the road (or go left for Picnic 11b). Almost immediately, go left on Rue des Puchots, climbing quickly to a T-junction, where you turn left (but *not* into Mont de la Crete, which is also on the left within a few paces). Keep walking, ignoring side turnings, until you come to a T-junction with a signpost pointing right to the 'Dolmen de Faldouët, 15yds'. This 50ft/15m-long prehistoric passage grave (**1h**) has a capstone reckoned to weigh over 20 tonnes.

Return to the road and bear right for some 200 yards/metres, to a distinct U-bend. The first opening on the bend carries a 'no through road' sign. Walk along it briefly, to get some marvellous views over Gorey Bay towards Mont Orgueil Castle, before returning to take the road on your left: it takes you down to the coast road, almost opposite **Gorey Castle** (**1h15min**). Visit the castle if you've time, or turn right and walk down to the shops and cafés of Gorey before catching your bus back to St Helier. Or retrace your steps to St Catherine's Bay.

Walk 12: ST LAWRENCE: THE HEART OF JERSEY

Distance: 4.8mi/7.5km; 2h40min

Grade: moderate, but with a few short steep sections

You will need: sensible shoes, long trousers

How to get there and return: 🚌 7 or 7b to St Lawrence's Church or 🚗 (ample roadside parking near the church parish hall)

Alternative, longer walk: St Lawrence circuit and the Jersey War Tunnels (9.6mi; 15.5km; *allow 5h-6h30min*; moderate; access as above). This walk is easily linked with Walk 13. Follow this walk to the crossroads at the 2h15min-point. Instead of turning left, go straight on here, then bear right after a couple of minutes where the road divides. Now keep straight on to join the start of Walk 13 at the Jersey War Tunnels, which are shown in the bottom left-hand corner of the map. After completing Walk 13, retrace your steps to the crossroads and turn *right*, to complete this walk.

This walk is a circular route winding along sheltered country roads, 'green lanes' and footpaths in the heart of Jersey. Before setting off, the parish church of St Lawrence is worth a visit; it stands on high ground and has a distinctive outline with a saddle-back roof to its tower. Just to the right of the church is the parish hall.

Start out at **St Lawrence**: take the lane with the 'no through road' sign, opposite the parish hall and war memorial. This descends very steeply down **Mont Misère** (Misery Hill), into the picturesquely-wooded St Lawrence Valley — known locally as '**Waterworks Valley**' on account of the reservoirs running the length of its stream (**15min**).

Reaching the bottom of Mont Misère, you will see your route on your left, just below road level — the wooden zigzag boardwalk shown overleaf. But before setting off along this path, cross the road and follow a signposted footpath to the right for some 100 yards/metres. Beyond a pump house, in a clearing among splendid horse chestnut trees, is the **St Lawrence Millennium Standing Stone** (one of twelve — there is one in each parish) and an information board which explains the natural history of the area and how a team of volunteers created a new '**Millennium Path**' to celebrate the year 2000. (The path continues down the valley, to Millbrook Reservoir further downstream, and also links up with 'green lanes' leading to St Helier — an option you might like to explore another day.)

Now retrace your steps to the zigzag boardwalk (also part of the Millennium Path) and follow it over the water meadow. Soon you cross a bridge and then climb 70 steps to a **viewpoint** among the tree-tops, high above **Danne-marche Reservoir**, from where you can look out across the narrow valley. This sheltered little eyrie is filled with wild flowers and bird-song in spring, full of butterflies in summer, and carpeted with fallen leaves and chestnuts in autumn. Depending on the season and time of day, you may get a glimpse of a red squirrel.

The path descends and returns to the road (**50min**). Turn left and continue along the valley for less than 100 yards/metres — until you see a narrow passageway cut through bedrock on the left. This is the path, and you will cross more bridges as it twists among trees and lush vegetation — ferns, honeysuckle and prickly butchers' broom and gorse. Beyond a grassy roadside picnic area with parking (**1h05min**), the route continues by crossing the road and running along the edge of a meadow.

Walk up to see the buildings of the Hamptonne Country Life Museum (open at irregular times; telephone 01534 633300 for details). To get there, leave the path and follow the road to the left, straight up the hill for about 300 yards/metres, then turn right; you'll see them on your right. And be sure to take a look at the lovely *colombier* (dovecot) on the left at the top of the hill.

The zigzag boardwalk over the often marshy water meadow

After your visit, retrace your steps to the path you were on and continue north. Cross a footbridge and go through a gate, once again crossing a road. With the stream beside you, the lane soon passes by an old **watermill** now converted into a house (**1h15min**).

From here the walk follows lanes, with a final stretch of pathway ending opposite another water-pumping station below yet another reservoir (**Handois Reservoir; 1h25min**). Follow the road as it winds to the left and ascends; at the top, take the turning on your right. On reaching the main road (A10) again, turn right and after about 100 yards/metres turn left, down Rue de la Golarde (**1h40min**). Turn left at the junction and enjoy the trees arching overhead (the 'tunnel' effect is dictated by ancient laws governing annual hedge-cutting). Go straight on as far as a small crossroads, bear right, and cross into a tiny lane, then cross another road, the B39 (**1h55min**).

Beyond the entrance to a manor house the lane twists and turns, passing an old water pump. Go straight on where the lane narrows, then turn right opposite a large farmhouse with a thatched roof. At a small crossroads among fields turn left; then turn left again at the next crossroads (opposite Leda House; **2h15min**). On your left is **Morel Farm**, (National Trust for Jersey), with a rare cobbled yard — a timeless scene viewed through the arched gateway. Go on down the hill to Le Rat, a tiny cottage beside another stream which runs through a quiet valley. Look out for **La Fontaine St Martin** — a stone well beside the road (**2h25min**).

Keep the meadow stream on your right as you go up a short steep hill and, at the next crossroads, turn right along another shady lane which will return you to the church at **St Lawrence** and the bus stop or your car (**2h40min**).

Walk 13: JERSEY WAR TUNNELS

Distance: 4mi/6.5km; 2h10min

Grade: easy

You will need: stout shoes

How to get there and return: 🚌 8a or 🚕 to Jersey War Tunnels (ample free parking). (Bus users also have the option of returning by bus from The Living Legend or the Victoria pub.)

Short walk: since this walk makes a figure of eight, a pleasant stroll of about half the length, mostly on footpaths, can be achieved by cutting out the loop between the 25min- and 1h50min-points.

First-time visitors to Jersey are often surprised to discover the extent and legacy of the five-year Occupation (1940-45). The story is no more vividly told than at the Jersey War Tunnels, a massive complex built when the Germans entrenched themselves in the Channel Islands, believing them to be stepping stones to a full invasion of the UK. A visit to the tunnels will amaze you. Hitler never felt the island sunshine himself, but his command HQ was not far away, where 'The Living Legend' theme park now stands. Everything remains as it was when the occupying forces left. This major tourist attraction vividly brings to life the incredible achievement of the architect and slaves who worked in appalling conditions to complete the project. The entry fee includes various multi-media exhibitions. The walk passes the entrance; allow extra time if you'd like to visit it.

Begin at the **Jersey War Tunnels** bus stop. Walk up Mont du Rocher, with a view to the museum entrance on your right. A minute or two later, follow the road as it makes a near-90° turn left, and come to a T-junction with Rue de la Ville au Bas. Turn left again, then go right, gently descending. Just after a sharp bend to the left, follow the

footpath signs on the right to avoid the narrow (but busy) main road near the **Victoria pub** (**25min**).

Go up the hill to the right, continue on La Route de L'Aleval (you'll see the road name on a stone), passing (on your left) the entrance to a war-time tunnel. This was once

Jersey's main mushroom farm, but is now defunct (mushrooms are imported from Guernsey). Walk on the grassy verge at the edge of the road for about 0.6mi/1km; there are more tunnel entrances on both sides of the road, now blocked. You are on a road that was created by the German forces for access to their military headquarters.

Turn left at the top of the hill at Le Pissot (**50min**) and soon reach **The Living Legend** (**1h05min**). The nerve centre for the Occupation was underground here — it's now incorporated into the buildings. During the war the command bunker was disguised as a cottage; today it is used as a store behind the scenes and is not open to the public. You can visit the attraction if you wish, (no charge if you do not choose to see the audio-visual presentation) but the walk continues by turning left just beyond The Living Legend, onto a very quiet road. Keep ahead until the road makes a sharp left turn and zigzags downhill, back to the **Victoria pub** (**1h35min**).

Turn right and go along the valley road about 200 yards/metres, to the millpond (on your left). From here the walk continues on footpaths. First there is a path through National Trust for Jersey woodland to **Quetivel** (**1h35min**), a restored water mill (open to visitors on Saturdays in summer). Across from the mill, the path goes through gateposts and continues downstream along the valley. Soon turn left to cross the stream, then go right along the roadside path as far as a **pumping station**. Cross the road carefully here, then take the steep path on the other side. This winds its way through the trees, over the hill and down to your car or the bus stop at the **Jersey War Tunnels** (**2h10min**).

The corridors of Jersey War Tunnels extend for more than a kilometre and were constructed by forced labour between 1941 and 1943, initially as a bomb-proof munitions store and repair facility. Between late 1943 and 1945 the complex was converted into a clearing station for military casualties, which in the end was never used.

Walk 14: GOREY VILLAGE AND QUEEN'S VALLEY

See map page 47

Distance: 4mi/7km; 1h55min

Grade: quite easy, with an initial climb of 200ft/60m

You will need: stout shoes (the reservoir paths are loose grit)

How to get there and return: 🚌 1, or 1b to/from the terminus at Gorey (Gouray), or 🚢 to/from Gorey harbour (paycard required)

Short walk: Queen's Valley Reservoir circuit (2mi/3km; 45min; easy). Walk the perimeter of the lake, possibly using the causeway to cross from one side to the other and achieve a figure-of-eight. 🚌 3a to Queen's Valley (St Saviour's Hospital) or by 🚢 (free parking at the St Saviour's Hospital end of the reservoir, or at the southern end).

Jersey's newest reservoir, resulting from the flooding of Queen's Valley, makes an enjoyable walk, because you can get around the entire lake on wide, mainly-level paths, encountering no traffic whatever. You'll also enjoy walking along quiet roads around Gorey.

Start in **Gorey**: walk up the B30 (St Martin's) road for about 250 yards/metres, but then take the U-turn to the right onto the coast road (B29). When you are just about level with Mont Orgeuil Castle, turn left. (Immediately left at this junction is a granite stone inscribed 'T.R. DE GRUCHY, CONNETABLE 1931'.) Almost as soon as you've turned off the main road, ignore a cul-de-sac on the left, then bear right, and stay on this road for half a mile (just under 1km), as it climbs quite steeply. You'll have magnificent views of the bay, Gorey Castle and also — on a clear day — the coast of Normandy. As the road levels out, ignore a left turning marked 'Public footpath and steps to Gorey village ½' (**20min**).

A few minutes later arrive at a junction where you have an opportunity to take a right turn (signposted 'Dolmen') and make a short detour to visit the **Dolmen de Faldouët** burial chamber (see Walk 11, page 52). Returning to the walk route, continue until you rejoin the B30 which you followed briefly at the start of the walk. Cross this main road to a continuation of the road you have been on. Then, after less than 100 yards/metres, turn left at a T-junction. (A right turn here leads after some 150 yards/metres to a large undercover garden centre with an excellent restaurant serving snacks or full-scale meals.)

You are now on the the B28; after about ten minutes (**50min**) come to the northern entrance to the **Queen's Valley Reservoir**. Here you have the option of walking along whichever side of the lake you prefer. I describe the path to your left, along the eastern side, but the path to the right on the western side is equally pleasant.

View from the path on the eastern shore of the lake (near Picnic 14)

Within ten minutes come to a causeway; not far beyond it, there is a grassy area on the left (Picnic 14; photograph above), where you can enjoy the view. Continue along the path, which now leads through a pleasant tree-lined stretch, eventually reaching the **dam** (**1h10min**) and overflow control tower at the southern end of the lake. This is just under a mile (1.5km) from the northern end of the reservoir.

Descend a steep winding path with steps and pass the water company's pumping station, to reach Le Chemin des Maltières. Here turn left, passing the **Mill Pottery**. Ignore a turning that forks back to your left; keep straight along. After ten minutes the road bends sharply to the right and then, almost immediately, it heads left again. Now you'll again enjoy fine views of Mont Orgueil Castle in the distance. At **1h30min** come to La Rue Horman and turn right. Within a couple of minutes, you will see the sign for the **Jersey Pottery** on your left. There is no admission charge, and this pottery is well worth a visit at some point during your stay; like the garden centre already mentioned, it too has an excellent restaurant. Also here is to be found an art gallery offering exhibition space for local artists.

Reaching the end of the road, turn left into another road with a 'no entry' sign. This takes you to the main street of Gorey village. It's a pleasantly picturesque area with a few shops and a post office. Continue along the road; it takes you back to the lower end of the B30, not far from where the walk began. Turn right and go down the hill into **Gorey**, to your bus or car (**1h55min**).

Walk 15: LA HOUGUE BIE

Distance: 3.5mi/5.5km; 1h15min

Grade: very easy

You will need: stout shoes

How to get there and return: 🚌 3a or 🚗 to La Hougue Bie (free parking); return the same way.

Short walk: La Hougue Bie — La Franche Ville — La Hougue Bie (2mi/4km; 55min; very easy; access as above). Follow the main walk to La Franche Ville (35min), then use the notes at the foot of page 61 to shorten the circuit back to La Hougue Bie.

I would usually apologise for suggesting a walk which stays predominantly on metalled roads, but in this case I won't. Not only do these lanes see little traffic, but they reveal a few Jersey peculiarities. And you wouldn't want to miss those, would you?

Start out at the fascinating site of **La Hougue Bie** (Picnic 15). Its history goes back to Neolithic times, but became more colourful with the passage of the years. The centre of attention here is a high mound (40 feet/15 metres), excavated only during the 1900s, revealing a burial chamber which you can inspect by stooping along a narrow passage for some 50 feet/15 metres.

On top of the mound are two chapels of 12th- and 16th-century origin. You can learn all about them in the information centre, which has a useful book section and modest refreshment facilities. There are also geological and archaeological exhibits here, as well as a memorial to occupation slave-workers housed in a wartime bunker which was once the German battalion command post for the eastern sector of the island.

Coming out of La Hougue Bie, turn right and then right again at the *second* crossroads (under **10min**). You pass

An old Jersey custom: 'marriage stones', built into the homes of newly-weds. They are to be found all over the island, but those illustrated above can be seen on the short version of this walk.

the magnificent house and driveway of La Hougue Grange, on your left. No more than ten minutes later, look out for a lane on your right, just before the road makes a 90° turn left. Head along this lane and bear sharp left. Continue for ten minutes, until you can bear right on another lane. Along here you'll start getting magnificent views towards Grouville Bay. Drop down into a small valley and climb gently out of it. Come to a road and turn right, alongside La Franche Ville, which has a fine granite wall worth seeing in its own right.

Where the wall ends, turn left on a short stretch of untarred road. Then turn right and quickly left (**35min**). *The Short walk keeps straight ahead here; see footnote below.**

Keep right where this lane forks, to gain a view over St Clement's Bay. Come to a T-junction and turn right, passing Highstead on the left. Bear left beyond it. After a quick succession of right, left and right turns, come to Prince's Tower Road. Turn left here and continue for a few minutes, then go right into La Rue des Friquettes. You pass St Michael's Preparatory School on the right and soon see La Hougue Bie to the right.

At the next junction, come upon a Methodist church and turn right on a road. To see the **marriage stones** shown above (they are on the Short walk route), bear right for a few minutes at the next junction: the first is set beside a gate on your right; the second into a wall on your left. Then return to this road, pass La Commune (a three-storey house, noted as an early producer of Jersey cider), and regain **La Hougue Bie (1h15min)**.

*For the Short walk, keep ahead here, to a crossroads. Go straight over on a road which eventually descends gently and turns to the right. Now look out on your right for a wall into which is set the 'marriage stone' shown above right. Further along, on your left, beside a gate, is the stone shown above left. Notice, too, the open brook beside the road: most brooks in Jersey are covered over, so that motorists don't bumble into them… Continue along the road to a right turn and head back past La Commune to La Hougue Bie.

61

BUSES AND INTER-ISLAND TRANSPORT

BUSES

The official island bus services ('**mybus**'; www.mybus.je) are operated by Connex Transport Jersey Ltd. Recognise these buses by their colour — pale blue. Although a few bus stops are marked by signposts, most are indicated by markings on the road surface. Always wait at a bus stop: *drivers will not pick up passengers at intermediate points.*

Because the services are so numerous, it is not possible to print full timetables in this guide. Instead, destinations are shown and the principal route number(s) serving them — note that where two or more services are shown, some will be weekdays only; some may be Sundays only. The listing includes not only the starting points for all the walks, but some of the island's tourist attractions as well. *A very approximate frequency* of services indicating the average time between buses is shown, but even so, there will be considerable variations. (Only on the St Helier to St Aubin weekday route are services sufficiently frequent to make it worth while waiting at a bus stop without consulting the timetable.) Note that the service is often more frequent between 9am and mid-morning, and again from mid-afternoon until about 6pm. Note also: the details shown opposite are for **summer services** (30 May to 2 October). At other times of the year, be sure to obtain the winter timetable, which is much more restricted.

Where the service is so irregular that it is impossible to give an average timing, no frequency is given; *refer* to the timetables. Be aware that changes in service numbers and timings can take place at short notice. *If you plan to make use of the buses, it is essential to obtain a copy of the current timetable from the St Helier bus terminus.*

OTHER BUS SERVICES

Connex also operates the '**myExplorer**' network — four routes (red, blue, yellow and green; see opposite) which run throughout the summer providing services to the island's key bays and attractions. These buses are also in the Connex pale blue livery, and the Connex range of unlimited travel passes is valid on both the Mybus and myExplorer services. Same website: www.mybus.je.

There are also frequent regular coach services called '**Easy Link**' (www.jerseycoaches.com), but these are *not* included on the facing page. Their vehicles have green and yellow livery. This competing service also calls at some island attractions and bays.

Destination	Route(s)	Approximate frequency	
		Weekdays	Sundays*
Airport	15	20-30min	30-45min
Bonne Nuit Bay	4, yellow	1h	1h
Corbière, La	12, blue	45min-1h	1h-1h30
Devil's Hole	7	1h	none
'Durrell' (Jersey's zoo)	3a, 3b, 23, green, yellow	30-45min	30-45min
Etacq, L'	12a, red	30-45min	1h
Gorey and the castle	1, 1a,1b, green	30min	30-45min
Green Island	1	30min	45min
Grève de Lecq, La	9, red	1h	1h
Grosnez (castle about a 10min walk)	8	2h	none
Hamptonne Farm (near)	7, 7b, yellow	1h	refer
Hougue Bie, La	3a, green	30-45min	1h
Jersey Lavender	blue	1h-1h30min	1h-1h30
Jersey Pearl	12a, red, blue	30-45min	1h
Jersey Pottery, Gorey	1, 1a, 1b, green	30min	30-45min
Jersey War Tunnels	8a, red, yellow	45min-1h	45min-1h
Kempt Tower	12a, blue	30-45min	1h
Landes Racecourse, Les	8	2h	none
Lion Park (Jersey Goldsmiths)	7, 7a, 7b, yellow	1h	refer
Living Legend, The	8a, red, yellow	45min-1h	45min-1h
Mare Wine Estate, La	7, yellow	1h	refer
Mielle de Morville, La	12a, blue	30-45min	1h
Old Portelet Inn	12	1h30min	refer
Pallot Steam Museum (near)	5	1h30min	refer
Plémont	8	2h	none
Portelet Bay	12	1h330min	refer
Queen's Valley Reservoir	3a, green	30-45min	1h
Rozel Bay	3, green	1h	1h
St Aubin	9, 12, 12a, 14, 15, blue	10-15min	20-30min
St Brelade's Bay	12, 14, blue	30min	30-45min
St Catherine's Bay	1b	1h	refer
St John's Church	5	1h-1h30min	refer
St Lawrence's Church	7, 7b	1h	refer
St Mary's Church	7, 7b, yellow	1h	1h
St Ouen's Bay	12a, blue	30-45min	1h
St Ouen's Parish Hall	7b, 8, 9, red, yellow	30-45min	30-45min
St Peter's Village	9, 15	1h	refer
St Saviour's Hospital	3a, green	30-45min	1h
Sorel (walk from St John's)	5	1h-1h30min	refer
Treasures of the Earth	12a, red	30-45min	1h
Val de la Mare	9, red, yellow	30-45min	30-45min
Zoo ('Durrell')	3a, 3b, 23	40min	1h

*On bank holidays, the Sunday bus service operates.

TRANSPORT TO OTHER ISLANDS (OR FRANCE)

Enquire at the Tourism Offices in St Helier for details of possible day excursions to Alderney, Guernsey, Sark or France.

Index

Geographical names comprise the only entries in this Index. For other entries, see Contents, page 3. A page number in *italic type* indicates a map; a page number in **bold type** indicates a photograph. Both of these may be in addition to a text reference on the same page. 'TM' refers to the walking map on the reverse of the touring map. See also bus timetable index on page 62.

Anne Port 11, 20, *47*
Archirondel 11, 19, *47*, 52
Beau Port, Le 9, **11**, 14, 29, *30-1*
Belle Hougue, La 44, *TM*
Blanches Banques, Les *30-1*, 35
Bonne Nuit Bay 42, 44, 63, *TM*
Bouley Bay 11, 18, 44, 63, *TM*
Corbière, La 10, 14, 15, 29, *30-1*, **36**, 63
Corbière Walk **5**, *30-1*, 35, **36**
Coupe, La *47*, **49**
Couperon, Dolmen du *47*, 48, **49**
Croc, Le 21
Dannemarche Reservoir, Le 54
Devil's Hole 14, **16**, 17, 43, 63, *TM*
Douët de la Mer *47*, 48
'durrell' (see Jersey's zoo)
Elizabeth Castle 9, *25*, **28**
Etacq, L' 10, 14, 16, 40, 41, 63, *TM*
Faldouët, Dolmen de 20, *47*, 52, 58
Flicquet *47*, 50, **51**
Gorey (Gouray) **12-13**, 20, 22, *47*, 58, 59, 63
   Bay and Pier *47*, **12-13**, 63
Grand Etacquerel, Le 10, 16, 40, 41, 63, *TM*
Green Island 63
Grève au Lanchon, La 43, *TM*
Grève de Lecq, Là **14**, **15**, 16, 43, 63, *TM*
Grosnez (Gros Nez) 14, **40**, 42, 63, *TM*
Hamptonne Country Life Museum 53-5
Havre de Scez, Le 46, *47*, 48, **49**
Hocq, Le 21
Hougue Bie, La 11, 18, 20, *60*, **61**, 63
Ile au Guerdain, L' **29**, *30-1*, 32, 33
Jersey Lavender *TM*
Jersey War Tunnels (German Underground Military Hospital) 14, 17, *54*, *56*, **57**, 63
Jersey's zoo 18, **19**, 63, *TM*
Kempt Tower 11, 15, 38, 63
La Lande du Ouest 29, *30-1*
Landes, Les 41, 63, *TM*
Lion Park (Jersey Goldsmiths) **17**
Living Legend, The 17, *56*, 57, 63
Macpela Cemetery 18
Mare slipway, La 11, 46, *47*, 52
Marrioneux, Le 43, *TM*
Mielle de Morville, La 10, 16, 63
Mielles, Les **10**, 22, 35
Millbrook 14, 17; Millbrook Reservoir 53

Mont Orgueil 18, 20, *47*, **12-13**
   Castle *47*, **12-13**, 58
Monts Grantez, Dolmen des 39
Morel Farm 55
Moulin de Quetivel, Le 17, *56*
Nez, Le *54-5*
Noirmont 10, **15**, *30-1*, 32, **33**, **34**
North coast path 22, 40, 42-4, *TM*
Pallot Steam Museum **18**, 63
Petit Port, Le *30-1*, 36, 44, *TM*
Pinnacle, The 10, 40, **41**, *TM*, **cover**
Plémont 16, 42, **43**, 63, *TM*
Portelet, Le 14, *30-1*, 32, 34
   Bay **29**, *30-1*, 32, 34, 63
   Common 14, 29, *30-1*,
Ouaisné, L' 14, 29, *30-1*,
Queen's Valley Reservoir 11, 21, *47*, 58, **59**, 63
Rocco Tower *30-1*, 35
Rocque, La **13**, 18, 21
Ronez 10, 17, *47*, *TM*
Rozel 11, 18, 19, 42, 44, 46, *47*, 49, 63, *TM*
   Bay *47*, 48, 63, *TM*
   Moulin de *47*, **48**
   Woods **2**, 11, **20**, 46, *47*, 49, *TM*
St Aubin 14, 22, *30-1*, 35, 63
St Brelade 9, 29, *30-1*
   St Brelade's Bay 15, *30-1*, 63
St Catherine's Bay and Breakwater 18, 19, *47*, **51**, 52, 63
St Clement 21
St Helier 9, 14, 17, 18, *25*, **26-7**, 28, 62-3
   town plan *25*
St Lawrence 14, 17, 53, *54*, **55**, 63
   Millennium Standing Stone 53
St Martin's 46, *47*
St Mary's 14, 63
St Ouen's *37*, 39, 63
   Bay 10, 15, *30-1*, 35, **38**, 63
St Peter's Valley *56*, 57
St Saviour's Hospital 11, 20, *47*, 58, 63
Sergenté, La 15, *30-1*, 36
Sion 18
Sorel 43, **44**, 45, 63, *TM*
Trinity 18, 63
Val de la Mare, Le 10, 16, *37*, **38**, 63
Vallée des Mouriers, La 43, 45, *TM*
Vaux Cuissin, Les *37*, 38, **39**
Waterworks Valley 11, 17, 53